TAKE A JOURNEY
TO CALM

This is an IndieMosh book
brought to you by MoshPit Publishing
an imprint of Mosher's Business Support Pty Ltd

PO Box 4363
Penrith NSW 2750

indiemosh.com.au

Copyright © Ginny Hartley 2021

The moral right of the author has been asserted in accordance with the Copyright Amendment (Moral Rights) Act 2000.

All rights reserved. Except as permitted under the Australian Copyright Act 1968 (for example, fair dealing for the purposes of study, research, criticism or review) no part of this publication may be reproduced, stored in a retrieval system, or transmitted in any form or by any means, electronic, mechanical, photocopying, recording or otherwise, without the written permission of the publisher.

 A catalogue record for this work is available from the National Library of Australia

https://www.nla.gov.au/collections

Title:	Take a Journey to Calm
Subtitle:	A self–help guide for new mothers needing coping strategies for their babies and young children.
Author:	Hartley, Ginny (1977—)
ISBNs:	978-1-922542-80-9 (paperback)
	978-1-922542-81-6 (ebook–epub)
	978-1-922542-82-3 (ebook–Kindle)
Subjects:	FAMILY & RELATIONSHIPS: Parenting / Motherhood; Parenting / Single Parent; Life Stages / Infants & Toddlers; SELF-HELP: Emotions; Self-Management / Stress Management

Cover concept by Ginny Hartley.

Cover design and layout by Ally Mosher at https://allymosher.com

Cover images used under licence from Adobe Stock and Envato Elements.

Internal illustrations copyright 2021 Simone Sheehan at https://www.instagram.com/Simone.Sheehan.9/

TAKE A JOURNEY TO CALM

A self-help guide for new mothers and mothers needing coping strategies for their babies and young children

By Ginny Hartley

Not Rocking This Motherhood Gig?

(There IS a Way to Achieve Mum-ability)

Take a Journey to Calm

with

Ginny Hartley

Bachelor of Occupational Therapy, Dip Counselling and Human Service

Author of the Mumability blog

Dedication

For my family and friends – you're simply the best!

Your love, support and encouragement means so much to me.

And to mums everywhere – you're amazing. Just own it!

Contents

Foreword vii

Introduction ix

Part 1 Learn To Look After Yourself 1
    Meet Your Body's Needs 1
    Make Time For Yourself 9

Part 2 Learn To Be Yourself 19
    Be Clear About Your Values 21
    Learn How To Bond/Attach 29
    Be The Mum You Want To Be 38
    Be Yourself While Responding To Your Child 46

Part 3 Manage Your Emotions And Thoughts 55
    Manage Your Emotions 57
    Control Your Thoughts And Emotions Differently 69
    Problem Solving Relieves Stress 77
    Stand Up For Yourself 86

Part 4 To Be Calm, Learn To Be Present 95
    Be Tuned-in To Your Child 96
    Be Tuned-in To Others 105
    The Final Word 110

Acknowledgements 112

About the Author 113

Disclaimer 114

References 115

Foreword

THE gift of time is something shared by all humans. How we give it, share it and make it mean something to others besides ourselves is a delicate balancing act that mothers know only too well. As I write this I am busy being mum to an eleven year old boy who is in the background talking about a friend who hurt his feelings. At the same time I am checking my text messages to make sure everyone who is supposed to be at work today is there. This is all happening while I am on holidays. I wouldn't change any of it for the world but it hasn't always been like this. I was like the majority of mums I have come across in my work; I was a subscriber to the competent women's syndrome – the belief that we can have it all and do it all. Now perhaps some mothers can be like that for some or most of the time but these mums know their limits. They know how to prioritise and they know when to reach out to someone else for help. These are skills that even we ambitious career-type women need to at best refresh or at worst drop our guard and learn.

Author of this book, Ginny Hartley, is an experienced therapist who has worked with thousands of mothers and their babies. She is firstly a mother devoted to her two boys as well as to a loving and resilient partner. I have known Ginny for more than 13 years. As with all meaningful relationships, ours has evolved over time. We share many of the same values, including speaking up for what we believe in, and the importance of family. Consistently, across the years, Ginny has been committed to supporting new parents in being kinder and wiser – whether immediately after the birth of their baby or in its early years. This book represents the tried and true knowledge, skills and attitudes that has helped mums become better mums, to be the mum they wanted to be, to be less stressed, and to be the 'real them'.

A compilation of commitment and clinical expertise, this book is an effective guidebook for new and not so new mums.

Deborah Carrin, Bachelor Social Work
Manager of Hume Community Team

Introduction

NOT enough time in the day. Feelings of inadequacy. Overwhelming tiredness. Crazy emotional roller coasting. Shattered self-confidence. A feeling that everything is out of control. Concerns and self-doubt mounting crazily. Feeling a failure. Striving to be the best. Worrying non-stop about the baby. Questioning your fitness to be a mother. Concerned you're not bonding with your baby. Distraught that your baby won't sleep. And that's just the half of it. They never told you that motherhood was this tough.

But wait – there's more! For today's mums the pressures certainly don't stop with the issues of new motherhood. Other stressors include the demands of motherhood competing with the demands of a career. There are parenting challenges, issues with domestic matters, finances, and important relationships, to name a few. You're trying so hard to be the perfect mother/partner/daughter/friend (as portrayed by media celebrities) and your apparent lack of success is weighing heavily upon you. Additionally – if you're like most women – you are trying to be everything to everyone. You feel as if you're a bad juggler – dropping all the balls of modern life – children, work, relationships and your own needs.

Are you too embarrassed to seek help? Have you secretly Googled for books that might help but can't find what you're looking for? Well, here's help: here's light at the end of tunnel!

Out of the chaos there can be calm. Take the journey. Start by learning about yourself and what drives you to be the way you are. Discover what underlies your unique triggers points. Along the way, you'll find out about your blind spots, and what you can do to ensure they don't get in the way of your emotional needs. Travel surely towards achieving a state of calm. Reading this book requires an active commitment to practicing skills discussed along the way. If you do this, you'll learn what is important to your wellbeing and what gets in the way of feeling calm.

I've been working exclusively with mums for many years in the public mental health system and more recently in a private practice, working specifically at helping mums adjust to life stressors. I'm all about identifying what gets in the way of putting yourself first, and then actioning new strategies that aim to reduce stress. Reframing how you think about your reaction is the key to success. We will unpack the barriers to finding your parenting mojo, and show you how to adopt new habits that help foster wellness and achieving balance in your life roles. You will learn how to manage difficult emotions, to check the facts on self-critical thinking and to target unhelpful behaviours that are getting in the way of you achieving a state of calmness.

Come take the journey to calm with me …

Ginny Hartley

PART 1
LEARN TO LOOK AFTER YOURSELF

It's a necessity – not an indulgence

Chapter 1

Meet Your Body's Needs

Don't be a human sacrifice

MOST mums look after everyone else before they think about themselves.

Why do we do that? Is it a female thing? An instinct? A maternal reflex? Usually, from the moment you are pregnant and you are aware of the baby growing inside you, relying on you for its survival, there is a shift in your attention from yourself to this other being.

All too soon you find yourself caring for a newborn – navigating the baby's feeding and sleeping routines, carrying out the multitudinous chores that go hand-in-hand with having a baby. Probably you're also trying to run a household, deal with 101 other demands upon you, and cope with extreme exhaustion. In the midst of all this upheaval, the last thing you're thinking about is yourself and your needs.

While feeling depleted might be unavoidable in the early days of birth recovery and new parenting, attending to your body's basic needs is critical to your mental wellbeing. *Learning to look after yourself is the first step towards achieving a calm state.*

When air stewards gives instructions in case of a plane crash, they tell you to put on your oxygen mask first before attending to children and others around you. It's the same when you're a mother. You need to look after yourself or you will not be able to meet the needs of your baby.

Investing in what your body needs means reducing your emotional vulnerability, and managing your emotions effectively. You'll start feeling stronger and more capable.

The acronym PLEASE[1] is a way of remembering the ingredients we need to build a more robust physical self and to optimise emotional wellbeing.

Maintain physical hygiene

P is for physically making sure you attend to basic personal hygiene. Have a shower, brush teeth/hair and wear clean clothes. It's easy to say but not always easy to do! By doing these activities, we are telling ourselves that we care. You will feel refreshed after taking a shower and dressing in clean clothes, not those stained from yesterday's feeding mishaps and worse. You'll feel more in control.

Make a commitment to personal care. You CAN fit it into your crazy schedule. Maybe get up a bit earlier, do it last thing at night or use the time when another adult is around to watch the baby. Be prepared to grab any available time and *put yourself before others*.

Treat illness

L is for treating illness. It seems obvious but many a mother diligently takes her child to the doctor while ignoring warning signs of her own illness. Pregnancy is demanding on the body and it can leave you deficient in vitamins, with hormonal changes, and with injuries such as pelvic floor instability and lower back pain. If it has been a while or you've been ignoring symptoms of pain or illness, book in for a checkup with a health professional. Take any prescribed medication as directed. Rest when you show signs of illness. Not only will you recover more quickly, you'll also reduce the chances of a physical illness getting worse and requiring more recovery time. By attending to physical health symptoms, you optimise energy levels, enabling you to function at your best. If that's not enough to motivate you, consider that as you age life-threatening diseases become more common but if detected early can increase the chances of a cure[2]

Think about booking a double medical appointment to allow time for a more leisurely consultation. Commit out loud to someone else that you need to make a doctor's appointment. This helps with accountability – knowing someone will ask you if you have made that appointment yet. Don't let excuses get in the way of treatment attendance; without a healthy body, we don't have anything to draw on in times of stress.

Eat regularly

E is for healthy eating. It is common for mums to find themselves skipping meals or snacking on high energy foods to give themselves the energy hit they need to get "stuff" done. Planning and eating regular nutritious meals will keep your blood sugar levels and energy stable. The next time you prepare a meal for your child or pack school lunches, think about your own meal plan for the day. It's not just your body that needs food; it is also your brain. Without glucose, our brains can't think clearly and are prone to getting stuck in unhelpful thinking patterns with diminished problem-solving abilities. The brain uses one half of the glucose supply for the body.³ Cars don't drive without petrol; we can't operate without proper fuel. If you have not eaten for many hours, chances are you are running on adrenalin and will eventually fall in a heap.

Set up a routine of planning your own meals. Have easy meals or snacks on hand for times when you are on the go. Don't let forgetfulness or being time-poor get in the way of your missing meals.

Avoid mood altering substances

A is for avoiding mood-altering drugs and alcohol. What goes up must come down. There are no short cuts to feeling good. Generally, if the drug is not prescribed by a medical professional, you need to be aware of the risks. Illicit drugs offer short-acting feel-good reactions that leave you feeling worse when they wear off.

Employ moderation and care to decisions you make regarding drugs and alcohol. Consider beverages such as herbal teas and fresh juices and don't forget hydration. We are roughly made of 60% water⁴ so having a water bottle on hand reduces the chances of dehydration.

Optimise sleep

S is for sleep. Getting enough sleep is essential for functioning at your best. It's not so easy to achieve when you are attending to children or having trouble switching off but once the sun goes down and there are fewer distractions you need to grab the chance to sleep. Try to get yourself to bed at a regular time and know that any form of rest is restorative. Be kind to yourself on days when you are feeling extra tired. No one is immune to feeling awful when sleep deprived. Often, mothers report that their sleep patterns have changed after they have children. To make matters worse women actually need more sleep than men, approximately twenty minutes more as they use more of their brain through multitasking.[5] They report sleeping lighter and waking up more often, even after their child sleeps through the night. Whether you are up attending to children or unable to sleep, be willing to adopt strategies that help you feel rested (when your heart rate drops to steady resting rate). Know that stress hormone levels are sensitive to thoughts such as "I need to get to sleep quickly"!

That old phrase sleep when baby sleeps is well worth following up if you are missing sleep. You will restore some of the sleep debt lost the night before and prepare yourself for the coming night.

Exercise regularly

E is for exercise. One of the most effective ways to relieve stress and improve energy levels. If you are already exercising regularly then that's great and I encourage you to keep prioritising time in your schedule. For those who haven't hit the pavement for some time, those who don't consider it's their thing, and those who aren't motivated – don't be disheartened. Start by thinking about ways you can move around the house, and build up from there. Exercise is one of the few ways you can reduce adrenalin build up and also gain a natural high from those feel-good hormones released when the body is moving.

Any form of cleaning or walking is exercise and just a twenty minute stroll can clear the mind.[6] See a health professional for advice if you have limits to consider. Consider teaming up with someone else to help make it happen, whether it is to mind your child or to go with you. According to the better health channel, 39% Victorian women aren't active enough and claim parenting demands as a common excuse for not getting 30 minutes of exercise a day, which is the Australian guideline for men and women.[7] The good news is it is never too late to start, and the benefits for physical and mental health make it well worth prioritising.

Case in Point

A 32 year old single mother of three children under six years old recently separated from her husband of 10 years. She reported feeling on edge all the time. She said that single parenting was harder than she ever expected. She was up front that she was unlikely to be able to come back for counselling as she had no one to mind her kids, and she barely had enough time to get the basics done, let alone make time to sit down for an hour.

Her single-session therapy was targeted towards educating her about the importance of self-care while also validating the many demands she was carrying on her own.

She was responsive to the review of the PLEASE skills and surprised how many factors she was not implementing. She had not considered that those items had a direct impact on her mental state.

P—She said she always had a quick shower and this was easier since the kids were not babies.

L—She was physically well and minimised her low iron levels on her last blood test. We discussed how any time she is unwell it would impact on her energy levels and her patience. She needed to be realistic about her limitations when she was sick, and she needed to be mindful of the importance of rest even though she was a single parent and had more time constraints and sole responsibilities.

E–She said she had always skipped breakfast and it was not uncommon to find herself starving by lunch time. We discussed introducing a piece of toast/banana with morning coffee to kick start her metabolism and to deliver glucose to her brain.

A–She denied any alcohol or drugs issues. She did say that her GP had prescribed an antidepressant when her marriage ended, and she took it on and off. We discussed the importance of taking tablets as prescribed at a regular time to balance our brain chemistry. She decided that she didn't want to be on medication but would look into an iron supplement.

S–She laughed when asked about sleep, stating that she had not had a full night of uninterrupted sleep in 6 years. She conceded that she often got sucked into binge-watching Netflix when her kids were asleep as it felt like the only time she had to herself. She agreed that aiming to go to sleep by 11pm was sensible, and that she would be better off the next day.

E–She said she missed co-parenting when she could more easily make time to walk with a friend. She would look into asking her family to help with minding her children, or she could increase the time her kids saw their dad, so she had time to do something active instead of endless chores.

She was told to review the PLEASE skill whenever she feels strong emotions. This is a quick way to review her self-care and make her aware why those feelings had emerged.

To Recap:

Don't let your emotions be the boss of you! Reduce your

vulnerability by taking the time to meet your own needs. Don't sacrifice yourself to everyone and everything else.

Practice the skill of PLEASE (It's an acronym here, and not merely a polite request!)

- Set up a daily routine of first attending to personal hygiene
- Address physical health issues immediately
- Make time to eat regular nutritious meals each day
- Show caution when using mood-altering substances
- Optimise your sleep routine by being prepared to rest and get to bed on time
- Exercise regularly and find ways to move when you can't go outside
- Don't forget the importance of attending to your body's needs while taking this journey to calm.

Your Task

Your first task is to commit to practicing the PLEASE skill each day for a week and to reflect on what you do well and what makes you most vulnerable.

Next

In the next chapter you will learn more about how to optimise your time use and how your perception of time impacts on your sense of satisfaction.

Chapter 2

Make Time For Yourself

Give yourself a break

THE reality is even worse than you ever imagined – caring for children makes HUGE demands on your time. You find yourself working 24/7 to look after this tiny person. Inevitably high stress is placed upon your relationships – not only with partners but also with family and friends. You simply don't have enough time in the day for everyone and everything. Talk about stressors!

Mothers, in particular, report feeling dissatisfied with their management of time. They often chastise themselves for being unproductive. It's a sure route to stress. Interestingly, research found that implementing time-use strategies didn't necessarily reduce the perceptions of time pressure. Women have a tendency to complete multiple tasks together and then to reflect that time passed too quickly to get everything done.[8] Perception of time quickens when you have too many competing demands – not a lack of efficiency.

Here are a few more examples of stress-causing factors:

- ➢ Adjusting to new parenting
- ➢ Transitioning back to work
- ➢ Not completing household chores

> Trying to be more readily available for your child or children's needs

> Having friends/family saying they never see you

If you feel as if there aren't enough hours in the day, that you're being pulled from pillar to post, and that you're simply not coping, then your stress levels are probably through the roof.

Consider that you're being unrealistic with your expectations. Make a list of your daily expectations and work out how long it takes to complete each task. Compare it to the hours in your day. You'll probably be shocked to see how unrealistic your expectations are.

The first step to dealing with time management is to stop striving for perfection. Accept you can't always do everything you would like to do.

Free up space in your mind to prioritise what is essential. It's easier said than done. You need persistence and to remind yourself every time you catch yourself trying to squeeze in too much to your day.

Don't forget to include your "me time" into your already full schedule as it literally is one of the few things you can do to reduces stress and increase your productivity and energy levels.[9] We've talked about your packed timetable and now we're going to insist you make time for leisure. It's crazy – but it's also VITAL for your health.

Take the time to do a time analysis. It will be worth it! Learn where your time goes. This analysis helps validate where your time is spent and invites you to review your use of time.

Consider that there are roughly 12 productive hours in a day, with a recommended eight hours sleep a night (you wish!), and then there's the time taken to care for your child, and the time you spend in house management. Don't forget to allocate how much time you spend on leisure/me time.

> *I challenge you to complete a time use diary for one full day and night. Specifically record how long it takes to complete everything you do and how long you sleep.*

Your result will most likely show that you underestimate how long it takes to do each activity and also that you often multi-task.

It doesn't take a mathematician to draw a simple pie chart. It's a great visual aid to seeing the proportion of time you allot to different activity – child care, personal care, domestic tasks, leisure, sleep, and so on.

When we're time poor, we often turn to multi-tasking in an effort to save time. The jury is in – you don't save time by multi-tasking! You make more errors or you add time by moving back and forth between tasks. Additionally, it is more stressful when you multi-task. The act of doing one thing at a time causes less stress. Research into productivity when multi-tasking found it reduced productivity by 40% due to time wasted moving attention back and forth from tasks and it was harder to tune out distractions.[10] The impact was worse with more complex tasks. You can see why it is illegal to text and drive a car. Folding washing while watching television doesn't seem as challenging for your mind but it is still slower than the time it takes to do one task one at a time.

> *I challenge you to record the time it takes to do 3 tasks – one after the other. Then do them again at the same time and see how long that takes. See if I'm right!*

Let's consider the daily routine of a new mum caring for a newborn in the first few weeks. An average newborn takes about an hour to feed once. Add in another hour for nappy/clothes changes and settling after feeding. While the baby is awake it requires constant supervision until it falls asleep (if you're lucky). This cycle rotates every three to four hours across 24 hours. If the baby feeds for 7 cycles for a conservative 2 hours each block, that's 14 hours spent on the baby alone. That doesn't include your own personal care, eating, cleaning, and shopping – to name just a few of the other demands on you. Yet mothers chastise themselves for not being good enough!

Seeking support, such as help with the kids or out-sourcing the cleaning (whether you pay or use friends/family), suddenly sounds like a reasonable strategy when you look at the time it takes to care for a newborn.

We need to accept that we cannot do it all.

The only way to save time is to prioritise and delegate.

Learning to say no when you are at capacity can be tough, especially if you enjoy helping others or you feel guilty about saying no. You may tell yourself that you are being selfish or not managing well enough but saying no is the only way to stay on top of your workload.

Make time to organise what needs to be done. Schedule what you can do and where others can help you. It's a useful way to gain clarity on how you will use your time. For example, if you want to prioritise exercise, it takes planning to decide the best time to go while ensuring the kids are cared for.

Anything is possible with good scheduling and accurate time allocations.

Focus on being efficient with your time by prioritising what tasks are essential and what can wait. The time it takes to boil the kettle and brew a cup of tea could also be used to do five minutes of dishes. While you enjoy that cup of tea why not gather your thoughts to organise the rest of your day.

Breaking large tasks such as cleaning the house into smaller tasks allows you to make use of time available and not get caught up in delaying until you have more time or energy.

After you have completed a time use overhaul and carved out some time for yourself, you may need to reacquaint yourself with your interests and consider how you can engage in them when you have mere minutes instead of hours of free time.

Ask yourself what your interests are currently and were in the past? What interests would you like to undertake now? Some topics to get you started include sports, theatre, cinema, music, art, games, collectibles, pets, study, and reading. An interest can be anything that draws your attention and generally makes you feel good when you do it.

Leisure time is often seen as a low priority. It's the activity you do when everything else is done – although, let's face it, nothing is ever fully done in those first crazy months of maternity. Needless to say, making time for leisure is an essential ingredient in connecting to and making time for on your journey to calm.

When you first calculate the percentage of the day you spend with your newborn and doing other vital tasks, you'll think it's not possible to fit a leisure break into your timetable. But you can! Even if it's only a couple of minutes in the early days, grab hold of those few precious minutes. Maybe have a cup of tea or coffee, put your feet up and go to your happy place in your mind. You could repot a plant or zone out to your favourite sound track. You might be able to catch a Judge Judy episode (no one else needs to know), have a few moments on your iPad playing Candy Crush, or pull off a yoga pose or two. Just make sure you're by yourself. It's a short cut to reenergising.

Don't let yourself feel disheartened if the first time you try to overhaul your time use it falls flat. There are plenty of external factors that can interfere with the best laid plans. Take lack of motivation as an example of something that interferes with your plans. Time to clean presents itself when your baby finally falls asleep but perhaps you have no motivation to use the time productively. You'd prefer to simply do nothing rather than get stuck into the housework. Who says you can't take a break? You deserve to.

I often say to mums that they are like a triage nurse running a busy emergency department. Not everyone can be seen to immediately – and they don't need to be. It's the same with chores. Dishes done regularly are worth doing as old food scraps set like concrete. Floors, on the other hand, can wait. In the early days, babies require a lot of your time but they don't make a lot of mess. Sure, they create the most laundry you've ever seen and they can't do anything for themselves but they don't move about and leave their toys everywhere, or throw food from one end of the kitchen to the other, or have to be watched constantly so they're not crawling into danger. It's perfectly okay to collect clean washing straight from the basket that is waiting to be put away! The pile of clean washing in the laundry basket might not look the best (and in reality it doesn't take as long as you'd think to put it away) but when there are so many new demands on you, putting away laundry can easily be missed.

You'll have good days and not so good days and this is hard for those people who go into motherhood with organised systems such as a weekly deep clean, gym before work and so on. Houses also keep considerably cleaner when you are not there all week. Remind yourself that things are different now. Some days you might wake feeling painfully sleep-deprived or your baby is only content when they are pressed up against your chest. The goal posts must shift or you risk eroding what little motivation you have to get through what is most important – taking care of you and your baby. All that early holding and reassurance you're giving your baby is bonding, nurturing and literally building brain pathways. What could be more important than that? You can always catch up on cleaning (it's always going to be there, anyway) – as hard as it may be to sit amid the mess!

Maybe you've partnered up with a Type-A personality and you fear criticism about "what you have done all day?" It's a stressor for you because they can't possibly know what it is like to care for a baby unless they've spent a day in your shoes. Fight the urge to fill every moment preparing for your partner's return as that will rob you of the small windows of time for you. Jumping on your phone to return messages, surf your social media feed, or pack your baby in the pram for sleep time so you can walk instead of clean is how you carve out windows of time for yourself.

Case in Point

This 35 year old first time mum of a three week old baby reported feeling a sense of failure at not being able to breast feed. She said that, after its birth, her baby had spent a period in the special care nursery, which caused a delay with the commencement of breastfeeding. Her baby was unwilling to latch-on and had developed a clear preference for bottle feeding.

She reported feeling anxious, exhausted and overwhelmed by keeping on top of her around-the-clock commitment to using the breast pump every four hours across the day and night to provide her baby with exclusive breast milk. She reflected that if she can't breast feed, she was concerned that her baby wouldn't be getting all the nutritional benefits of breast milk. She said it was particularly difficult in the middle of the night to pump and to feed her baby. She felt shame about telling other mothers her baby was bottle fed. She said there didn't seem to be enough time in the day to get anything else done. For that reason she felt like she needed to stop wasting time attempting to feed her baby breastmilk even though it was contrary to everything she wanted to do for her baby. This conundrum was causing her enormous stress.

Her time use was analysed over a 24 hour period to help her see just how much time was being absorbed into feeding her baby. The time taken to pump, store milk, feed baby, settle the baby afterwards and clean all the equipment took on average 2 to 3 hours each time. She reflected that it was as if she were caring for twins. She had completely underestimated how much time was going into pumping. She decided to set a time frame on how long she would pump and that she would enlist the help of her partner and mother to help out with chores and some of the feeds to free up time to do other things. She also could see that her motivation to pump despite the demands it placed on her was her attempt to control the situation – with its origins possibly coming from her own mother's controlling behaviour. She saw it was unfair to blame herself for something that wasn't her fault.

To Recap

The first step to dealing with time management is to stop striving for perfection. Accept you can't always do everything you would like to do. The only way to save time is to prioritise and delegate. Anything is possible with good scheduling and accurate time allocations.

Ensure your daily schedule includes leisure activities/me time. It's vital to your health. Take up an old or new interest and schedule it into your time table.

Your Task

Do a time use analysis by keeping a time-use diary for a day and find out whether the time it takes to complete your activities fits with the time available.

Be prepared to acknowledge what is possible in any given day and delegate tasks to meet your time-use priorities.

Check in with your interests – because making time for leisure makes us feel good about ourselves.

Next

In the next chapter you will learn about the power of connecting with your values to understand what is important to you, and how your values dictate what motivates you and therefore what your priorities are.

Part 2
Learn To Be Yourself

Be the real you

Chapter 3

Be Clear About Your Values

Know what really motivates you

ARE you one of those people who sets New Year resolutions? Or do you think by setting goals you're setting yourself up for failure? Either way, we would probably all love to be the best version of ourselves, and would happily take up an achievable solution to get there.

We feel great when we first set a goal; we are full of motivation to succeed. This is not surprising because we are receiving an endorphin hit in the brain. We swing straight into action until we hit our first barrier (sometimes as soon as the next day!) Fear sets in and before we know it the goal falls by the way side. Then stress sets in because we see ourselves as failures.

We can always daydream, of course. Take a moment now. Give free rein to your imagination. Do you dream of being an amazing parent or are you dreaming of being happier, smarter, nicer, healthier or wealthier? Perhaps you dream of a fabulous new job, winning the lotto or going on holidays to an exotic location. Dreams are great but, for the moment, that's all they are. Hang onto them though; we all need dreams.

Who you are doesn't come from what you aspire to or what goals you set for yourself on New Year's Eve (or any other time). The first step in discovering who you are comes from working out what your values are. Your value system helps you live a life with greater purpose and meaning.[11]

Values work like a compass. They aren't tied in with achievement, yet they can steer you effectively towards what you want more of.

Did you know that we tend to be drawn to people with aligned values?

How do you work out what are your core values? A common method is to write your own obituary! While it sounds morbid it is an efficient way of distilling what's important to you. Ask yourself what you want to be remembered for. What do you want your kids to recollect about their childhood? This might feel uncomfortable as you tell yourself all that you could do better – whether it be how you clean or decorate your house, if you are a fun-loving parent, how you juggle work and life, if you are relaxed enough to enjoy life. From the "responses" you write you can see if you are meeting your values or not.

Before you think about it, here's a reminder not to regress to the old "I'm not good enough" story. Instead you have the tools to action change. For example, if you highly value family time you will now be aware of its importance to you, and you will be able to map out uninterrupted family time. Ditto for anything you value, such as health, exercise, serving nutritious meals, and so on.

Another way to discover what values you consider most important is to study a list of core values and notice which ones you are drawn to.

To help you see what motivates you (which in turn shapes how you parent) I'm going to ask you to choose which of these ten values stands out to you …

Calmness – being free of stress and having a sense of peace that comes from focusing inside yourself so that you feel relaxed or alert despite what might be going on around you

If calmness is what you crave then that will dictate how you spend your time and the choices you make. It might mean staying in a familiar job, not writing to-do lists, or making time for pleasure over productivity. Actively practise actions to help you feel calm, and seek out support to keep yourself in check.

Security – feeling safe and protected – financially, in relationships or physically.

If this is you, it might be hard for you to imagine being any other way. People who are free-flowing and impulsive might seem silly or reckless to you. Your past may also influence why security is important to you – whether you grew up without security or whether it was drilled into you. Actions such as keeping budgets, going to the supermarket with a shopping list to avoid purchasing unnecessary goods are important. Your partner choices will be carefully considered, any big decisions such as marriage are likely to be scrutinised, and having a child from an unplanned pregnancy is unlikely to happen.

Joy – feelings of contentment and happiness, which when focused upon is seen everywhere as a constant – through laughter, in enjoyment, and in pleasure with life and others.

For you, pleasure will be prioritised over other responsibilities. Routines are planned around activities you enjoy. You value feeling good. If you lack some joy in your life this might mean making more time for play, preparing your favourite meals, and making time for interests or social happening. The more you work on making time for some joy in your life, the more it becomes part of your routine.

Ambition – being driven and wanting to advance by having self-belief in your ability to succeed and achieve your goals in work and personal pursuits.

What a busy mind you have if you are all about achievement. Setting goals and reviewing progress sets you apart from the folk who sit around hoping it will happen without any action on their part. Less than ten percent of people actively pursue their goals; it takes a certain type of person to persist and to not let procrastination get in the way. By diligently breaking down goals into achievable actions and seeking out support early you keep yourself on a forward trajectory.

Health – being mindful of what you eat; how you move and sleep; how to look after your body to prevent disease and to promote wellness.

So many choices each day dictate how healthy we are. New research shows that genes can literally be turned on and off by modifying our health. If being healthy is important to you then self-control around healthy diet choices, sleep habits and exercise are prioritised. Perhaps it means you are prepared to leave a party early to get to bed, or that you seek out timely advice when a health issue arises and then follow the recommendations. You are motivated towards wellness and you seek out information about health for you and your family.

Education – an atmosphere where opportunities to advance self is encouraged through always learning through formal schooling and informal teaching.

Make time to learn. Homework is not a dirty word for you as you know that time spent studying pays off. It isn't a waste of time and by "doing your homework"/practicing what you have learnt, it becomes embedded in your routine. You seek out help when you need to and discover how making time to learn new skills makes you feel good.

Teamwork – working with a group of people to achieve a common goal ahead of their own individual talents and goals

Being able to ask for help and being able to see that we all have different skills is your mindset when it comes to teamwork. When a baby comes along you see it as being a team effort and not something for you to master alone. Early on you are able to ask for advice and practical support from others. In your job you have chosen to work in a team where collaborating is welcomed and the environment is open.

Freedom – believing that people have a right to choose and make their own decisions without being forced to do so.

This person is not going to be told how to parent and might find it easier to give herself time to adjust to new parenting in a way that works for them. You are not going to be dictated to by the rule of others, and you have strong self-determination when it comes to following your own instincts. For example if you want to breast feed until your child is five then that is what you'll do. Being able to step away from the herd and listen to your own voice is freeing for you.

Optimism – believing that things will turn out well in the end.

You are a glass half-full person. There is always something to be grateful for and you hold a strong belief that everything will work out in the end. This mindset motivates action to perceived problems, and an inner belief that tough times are temporary. It is a marker of resilience to see positives over negatives. That doesn't mean you are all Pollyanna and are not in tune with feeling sad and hopeless. You just don't let yourself wallow, and will seek out help and challenge yourself to see a way through the toughest of scenarios. For example a child born with additional needs or an unexpected death will be grieved for before you consider how to move forward.

Family – being an integral part of a group of people who are related to each other, or live together or share beliefs, and who all care for each other.

If this is you then you make time for these special people over everything else. You are the initiator of communication, catch ups, care giving and whatever is needed to be there. You may have been raised in a close family unit, in receipt of this care now, and it has been affirmed as invaluable. Or you may have come from the opposite and want something different for your family. Maybe you've added your own close friends to your version of family. It may also dictate other life choices you make such as turning down a job that will take you away from home. You might set up family rituals of shared meals and activities you do together to cement the importance of family to you.

Your chosen values tie in with how you parent, and through what you prioritise for your children. Let's look at some examples:

The ambition value might mean working in a certain type of job despite its long hours and demands, thus being a role model of the importance of hard work and also showing a positive self-identity to your children.

The health value might mean adopting a strict health diet, making time for exercise and stress management ahead of other leisure activities – which is teaching your children the importance of self-care.

The joyful value might mean you are more fully in the present and all about highlighting experiences that feel good ahead of what else needs to be done – teaching your child to find happiness in the small things and to find calmness through joy.

The security value may impact on where you live, and following a budget where affordability trumps instant gratification – teaching your child about responsibility.

So, the next time you're feeling defeated or you wonder why you feel so strongly about some things and not others, tap into your values to help understand what motivates you.

> **Case in Point**
>
> *This 38 year old mother of two children under four years old was on extended leave from her job working at Parks Victoria. She presented feeling depressed and unmotivated to do anything. She reported not enjoying being at home full time with her kids and feeling guilty about this. Each day felt like ground hog day to her.*
>
> *Counselling involved helping her to connect with her values as a means of understanding what might be contributing to her situation. She was passionate about the environment and had decked out her home with many sustainable features. Her face lit up when she spoke about the work she had done in the past such as leading a project to transform an abandoned waste land to a usable green space. She had not considered that, since she had her children, she had lost touch with the environment and the job she valued so much. This had contributed to her loss of wellbeing. She reflected that she needed to have purpose outside of the mum role to refill her tank, and this prompted her to review her position of sending her kids to child care.*

Additionally it made her realise how important it was to her that her children were raised to care for the planet. She started to brainstorm fun ways she could teach them – such as building a worm farm and eating nude food snacks.

Her blind spots had been the assumption that if they could afford for her to stay home she ought to be grateful. Her need for self-identity was connected to her working. She returned to part-time work, and her partner also made changes to his work schedule after he saw the transformation in her. She was so much happier to have a work life balance.

To Recap

Setting goals can lead to stress if we fail to meet those goals. Dreams are only that for now. Instead take the first step to discovering yourself by connecting with your values. To understand your values is to know what really motivates you.

Your Task

Check in with your values to understand what motivates you as a parent.

Next

In the next chapter you will learn about how the bonds you formed in your own childhood influence how you relate to your child, and what you can do about it to foster a healthy relationship with your child.

Chapter 4

Learn How To Bond/Attach

Strengthen the bonds with your baby

HAVE you ever thought about how you get along with others? Many of you will answer that you get along well with others. But how many of those people are you comfortable enough with to share your true feelings. No doubt the list has shrunk considerably.

We call the special bond we have with a precious few an "attachment". A secure attachment for an adult is defined as someone who is comfortable to be alone and who is also able to openly seek support and share their feelings.

Forming attachments begins at birth. One research pioneer[12], in his study of babies, noted they have an incredible knack, from birth, for seeking out their mothers. This is not just about hunger. Babies also seek attachment for meeting their social and emotional needs so they feel safe and also for comfort. This led to the conclusion that children are biologically pro-grammed to attach to one person, and the first two years are critical. Children can suffer irreversible damage if their needs are not met. The original researcher was driven to understand attachment to make sense of his own attachment issues. He was raised with minimal attention from his parents who feared they would spoil him, and so they spent minimal time interacting with him and sent him to boarding school at age seven.

Mums quickly tune in to the meaning behind the different cries their babies give – for attention, hunger, discomfort, and so on. For a secure attachment to form babies not only need consistency from their care-giver but they are also sensitive to how accurate and harmonious the care is in meeting their needs. (Yes, from day one the cunning little devils have you running to their bidding!) Here's an example of how a baby shows a secure attachment. When the care-giver leaves the room the baby starts to cry. It stops crying when the care-giver re-enters the room. The baby has learnt that the care-giver will return to meet the baby's need.

It is reassuring to know that the majority of babies, some 70%, are securely attached to their primary care-giver[13] Security is achievable even if parents only get it right about half the time. In another study, mums from low socioeconomic background with irritable babies didn't need to get attachment right all of the time but by responding properly as little as 50% of the time still created a healthy attachment.[14]

Aiming for perfection causes unnecessary anxiety and distraction from actually tuning into what your baby is trying to tell you.

The next time you feel a pang of guilt for spending an inordinate amount of time cuddling or playing with your baby ahead of carrying out other tasks, reassure yourself that you are laying down the most important social – emotional skills for your child. Just like building house foundations, it's hard to go back and fix insecure footings in later years.

> *I'm giving you permission to love freely and ignore fears of spoiling your baby with affection.*

During the first year of their life, babies rely heavily on their parents to build this emotional scaffold that makes them feel confident to express their needs and to receive care. Where the mother is emotionally unavailable or unreliable, the baby might learn to not show its full emotions. For example, the baby doesn't react to its mother leaving the room. This is known as an insecure (avoidant) attachment. Also showing an insecure (avoidant) style is a baby who exaggerates its needs by crying intensely to ensure its mother does respond. Another example is a baby who pushes its care-giver away. Each style accounts for approx. 15% of babies.

Early disruption to the bond between care-giver and baby impacts negatively on the adult's self-esteem and the baby's ability to grow up into a happy functioning adult.

Now, back to you! Knowledge is power. Reflect now upon your own upbringing and the attachments/bonds you formed. This will help you understand how you are set up to provide care. For example, if you didn't receive loads of physical affection growing up, you might feel overwhelmed or even irritated by a child that craves affection. Once you become aware of why you are feeling uncomfortable you can work on creating a different experience for your child.

Learning to regulate your emotions is tied to understanding what memories you carry of the care you received. This helps you to separate your reactions from what your baby is demanding from you.

Babies are hard wired to want to bond with their mother, and repair can occur at any time.

Let's work out what sort of attachment you have in your adult relationships and what you can do to help build a secure attachment with your child.

Here are some questions to ask yourself to determine your attachment style. There are three styles of attachment – secure, anxious and avoidant. We will also look at what you can do to support your child developing a secure attachment with you.

Securely attached parents say yes to the following questions:

- Is it easy for me to share my feelings with others?
- Am I emotionally available to meet other's needs?
- Can I regulate my own emotions whilst attending to another person's positive and negative reactions?
- I am curious about others needs and prepared to offer support?
- I seek out social support when I need it
- I have boundaries in place in close relationships?

Tips for securely attached parents

- Continue being a responsive tuned-in parent
- Be aware of separating off what you feel from what your child is feeling/expressing

> Make yourself available for quality time

> Show them that you love them with affection and kind words

This is the most straight forward attachment style to identify with. If this is you, it means your own parents raised you in an environment where your emotions were welcomed and validated. It is likely to come more naturally to you to parent this way toward your child.

It would be interesting to compare yours with your partner's attachment style. Your partner might be the same or be one of the following parents. Consider the impact that will have on co-parenting by reviewing the traits below.

You also don't need to be attuned all the time to building a secure attachment. Pay attention to what you are most comfortable with and what is challenging. For example, do you communicate your love through giving lots of physical affection or through soothing words or play-based actions?

Anxiously attached parents say yes to the following statements:

> I want to share my feelings but I worry others won't support me

> I don't like to be alone

> I over react to other people's distress and my feelings can get entwined

> I might over react to get attention when feel ignored

Tips for anxiously attached parents

- Notice when you are feeling anxious and name it as your emotion state
- Be prepared to pause and take a moment to settle yourself
- Be a detective and check out what your child needs
- Resist the urge to make this about you

Make time to debrief about your challenges to build a secure base.

It can be a real challenge coming face-to-face with your anxious self through parenting your child. Before kids you may have ignored it by keeping yourself busy, or you coped by choosing a partner or friends who supported you and made you feel secure. Early days of hearing your baby in distress or when attempts to sooth it are met with more crying are likely to set off your own anxiety and have you second guessing if you are doing something wrong. Being able to pinpoint your own anxiety response from that of your baby is critical to responding accurately to your baby's needs. Talking to someone else or watching how others respond can help you tune into what your baby is needing, and help you learn about normal infant behaviour.

Avoidant-attached parents say yes to the following statements:

- I don't like to share my feelings with others as I fear my needs won't be met
- I minimise my emotional reactions
- I am extremely self-reliant
- I might seem quiet or withdrawn at times

- I avoid and distance myself from someone who is too needy
- I feel proud of how well I keep it together
- I anticipate people will let me down

Tips for avoidance-attached parents

- Reflect and validate your child's expressed needs, whether they feel valid to you
- Openly show your child affection even when it feels uncomfortable
- Resist telling your child to go away or not to feel upset when they are upset
- Encourage your child to seek support

You might have been able to fool others in your life that you are not an emotional person but your baby's super power is eliciting a response from you like no one else has done before. The relationship is uniquely intense and your challenge will be to fight the resistance to minimise your child's emotions. From your own learning experience growing up, your mind will try to tell you there is something wrong with how intensely your baby is communicating its needs. Don't worry when your first response comes from old patterning. There is always scope for repair.

Case in Point

A 25 year old mother of two children presenting with concerns about not feeling bonded to her second born child, a boy. She said she felt an immediate connection when her daughter was born. She said it came naturally to her to respond to her daughter's needs. She said she had wanted to have a girl as she enjoyed a close bond with her mum. She was perplexed by her son. She said he didn't like to be held and it was impossible to know what he wanted, yet when her husband came home the son responded better to his father.

When she was observed interacting with her six-month-old son during a game of peek-a-boo she seemed reserved. She was mechanical in her actions and fixated on seeing the signs he was not enjoying the game. She missed his need for breaks and hence modifying the interaction. I pointed out that he seemed to like it when he can hold the cylinder. I modelled to her the same game but with me exaggerating my actions and making funny vocal sounds.

After a few play-based sessions with lots of direct modelling she related to some of the markers of avoidance, stating she does not like to show others she wasn't coping, and so had held back from her son by withdrawing into herself. With further exploration of where this pattern might have come from, she conceded that she had unconsciously held back from fully bonding with her son as she feared he would one day want nothing to do with her. In her own family of origin, father and son, and mother and daughter had been paired units, so she had assumed her family unit would be the same. With awareness she learnt to hold her fears and also to see what her son was trying to say – whether it was in times of playful laughter or when he was fussing.

To Recap

Bonds/attachments are formed at birth. How you react to that bond with your baby is influenced by the bonds created in your own childhood. You might have a secure attachment to your baby – or maybe an anxious attachment or an avoidant attachment. Tips were supplied to assist in adapting your style to meet the needs of your baby.

Your Task

Work out your attachment/bonding style and study the tips that will support you.

Next

In the next chapter you will learn how your childhood influences how you parent, and what you can do about it.

Chapter 5

Be The Mum You Want To Be

And be your own person, too

BY looking into our past, we can see the impact it has on how we react to our child.

Understand the relationship you had/have with your own mother and her mothering role. Making peace with it allows you the space to create and to build a healthy, secure and satisfying relationship with your child.

When you become a mum it is normal to experience memories of your own childhood. Perhaps you believe your mother was unavailable to your emotional needs. Or she smothered you with love, leaving you little space to be free and take risks. (Don't forget to consider the aspects of your mother's parenting that you loved!)

Prior to having children, you might have been able to overlook painful childhood memories. Yet, while experiencing postnatal challenges, suddenly unresolved issues from your past appear as flashbacks. Often, if you analyse it, those same issues are being played out in your parenting style.

Ghosts in the Nursery [15] is a pioneering book exploring this phenomenon. Painful memories are described as 'visitors' from the past that appear like uninvited guests interrupting interaction between a mother and her baby.

I often say to women, who describe feeling angry and let down by their mothers, to consider what type of mothering their mothers experienced. It makes it easier to understand why their own mothers behaved as they did. Certain behaviours are passed down through the generations. In almost all cases, though, our mothers were simply doing the best they could manage at the time.

You can break this chain, you know, to become the mother you want to be and not a reflection of past parenting.

Being able to reflect on positive and negative childhood experiences is a useful method for drawing out how you want to be the same or different.

> *Are you able to recall what books or nursery rhymes you enjoyed?

Perhaps you had a favourite book that was read over and over. You can share this with your child and create those meaningful connections for them. Likewise recalling that your parents were not available as they worked long hours or didn't make time to play with you can be turned into actions by doing the opposite with your children. We all think we are going to be better different at some point growing up. Its only when you get there yourself that you realise it isn't as easy as it looks. Maybe your parents worked because they didn't have a choice. Maybe they didn't play with you as it wasn't something they knew was important.

Being able to see the connections and name the times when you are repeating patterns is the first step in making change.

Breaking patterns is hard, particularly those passed down through generations.

> *Have you ever heard yourself repeat phrases you heard a lot of growing up?*

Some common examples are "money doesn't grow on trees", "knock it off", "your father can deal with you when he gets home" and "I'll wash your mouth out with soap". These types of statements can roll off the tongue with little conscious thought.

> *Do you find yourself comparing the toys you had as a child with the bountiful number of toys your child has?*

Thanks to the internet, children today are bombarded with advertising the latest toys. Plus the variety of toys is so much greater today. It is only natural to feel aghast at your child's expectations for Christmas and birthdays – and every time you shop!

It is important to make time to reflect on how you are going as a mum.

> *Do you feel like you are doing a good job?*

Pay attention to your self-talk and what you say to yourself when you go about the day. Do you acknowledge gains and consider what contributed to times where nothing seems to be going right. What do you say to people when they ask you how you are going? Your mindset and what you notice is what will determine the answer to this question. What others tell you can also be highly influential.

> *Are you happy with the relationship you have with your mum?*

(Whether she is present in your life or is no longer there due to death or conflict, her impact will be present.)

Whatever the relationship you have, it is going to play a role as you find your own mothering shoes. If you are close she will likely be present to offer support, guidance and help you transition more easily to this new role. In contrast, her absence may be felt during times of isolation, fatigue and feeling overwhelmed. During your young adult years when you were busy pursuing your own personal goals, whether it be a career or travel, life can be so busy that there is little time to ponder where your relationships stand with our parents. A loss of a parent in the past can be felt in a new kind of grief as you imagine what life would be like now if they were still here. It can be painful and also deeply therapeutic to acknowledge the grief and find a way to honour some aspect of the way you were raised. It could be a song, a meal or activity you enjoyed together ...

> *Do you ever regret the way you respond to your child? (Such as feeling impatient with their endless needs, raised your voice, and so on.)*

That pang of guilt usually follows a moment of parenting that you regret. We are not robots and can't always respond in the way we aspire to. One of the quickest ways to feel disappointment is to set yourself a goal such as I won't lose my temper today, only to be disappointed the moment you do. A more constructive approach is to make note of what happened before you lost your temper as there is likely to be a pattern. So cast your mind back over the last few weeks and pinpoint any moments that have been hard and led to you getting angry.

> *Do you ever blame your past as justification for current issues?*

While our past provides critical early programming and shaping it does not let you off the hook for considering what role you played. Blaming others might make us feel vindicated for a moment but it is short lived because the pattern repeats. Of course acknowledge where you learnt to respond the way you did as it will help you understand why. Take for example the common expectation a generation or two ago for children to be seen and not heard. During that era of parenting it was okay to smack your child to assert your authority. New age parenting has taught us that all behaviour has meaning. If the child is shut down then the need is internalised.

Why not talk to someone you trust to help you unpack the issues you have with your mother and the parenting style you want to adopt. Or you could journal or meditate or self-talk. Maybe you can have open discussions with your mother about how you want things to be. At first it may be uncomfortable to come face-to-face with your mother's voice in your parenting, so remember that having the knowledge is half the battle.

Being your own kind of mum doesn't mean your whole life needs to pivot around this role. I reiterate the importance of making time for your *own* interests, those you enjoy and that make you feel good. If you have let your hobbies lapse or have lost touch with friends who don't have kids, consider this is a good time to reconnect with that part of you. (Right now – while reading this chapter!) Time away engaged in other things not only gives you a break but also contributes to your self-confidence. It also contributes to your building a revised self-identity, including your role as a mother and all the other roles that make you unique.

Be bold and own your own version of being a mum. Don't let society or the people around you define how you parent.

> **Case in Point**
>
> *To pay the mortgage, a 28 year old mother of one year old toddler recently returned to part-time work in a job she didn't enjoy. She said she resented the need to return to work for financial reasons before she was ready. She felt anxious and guilty each time she dropped her child at child care. She said she had dreamed of becoming a mum since she played with her dolls on her own as a child. She had steered away from focusing on her career as she didn't want her own child to feel like a hindrance.*
>
> *Exploration of her own past history highlighted that she was not close to her own mother, and this had been more pronounced since she had her own baby. She was disappointed that her mother had not scaled back her work to spend a day minding her first grandchild.*

The client doted on her child and responded to her every need. A friend told her recently she was too soft and she was raising a little princess. She felt hurt by this judgement and reasoned that this woman was cold hearted and jealous.

Counselling explored what sort of work would be meaningful to her, and she decided to do a course in child care so that she could run a family day care from home. This would allow her to make money and still to be the hands-on mum she desired to be. She accepted that she could not change her mother. She had her own way of showing she cared when my client was young – by taking the family on exciting holidays. The client said she could not imagine her mother, who was a doctor, being anything other than a career person. The client realised that it was not okay to be the type of mum hers had been.

The client's blind spot was not making any time for her own interests. She had loved hiking before becoming a mum, and she decided it was important to make time for herself, and so she joined a hiking club.

To Recap

We can look into our past to see how we react to our own child. We often continue the parenting styles of our mother and her mother before her. Don't be part of a chain that didn't make you happy when you were a child. Alternatively incorporate those aspects that you loved. Be bold and be your own version of being a mum. Don't let society or the people around you define how you parent.

Your Task

Consider your childhood relationship with your mother. What did you like about it? What are the things you wished she'd done differently? What makes you angry about her parenting style? Can you decide why she did those things? Look at the things she did that you want to do differently or to replicate with your child.

Next

In the next chapter you will learn how to separate what is happening for you and your child. Learning to tune into what your child needs and how their unique personality communicates those needs will help you be a calmer mum.

Chapter 6

Be Yourself While Responding To Your Child

They have their own personality from the start

BE sensitive to your child's needs without muddying the water with your own reactions.

To achieve this sensitivity you need to reflect on how you parent. It's tricky! It involves being able to stand apart from yourself to observe yourself. It's a process of learning to hold your own opinions and actions and someone else's at the same time. Research tells us that strengthening a parent's ability to do this helps build that secure attachment we talked about earlier. The result is you'll enjoy a greater level of positive connection with your child. And you are also providing early role modelling for your child's future ability to deal with strong emotions and his/her understanding of them.

After reading the previous chapter you are aware that the way you were raised influences your automatic parenting responses. It makes sense that if you were raised in a calm caring household, it is easier for you to be calm – as opposed to being raised in a house of tension and heated arguments that taught you it is okay to express yourself with strong words. Similarly, if you learnt that children must respect authority or suffer the consequences, it will be harder for you to consider the new age idea of validating all emotions.

It may be difficult to always remember that every emotion felt by your child needs to be validated – even if the way they expressed it is driving you bonkers. To help you do this we need to understand that everyone, including babies, has their own unique personality – which is often described as 'temperament'.

It's easy to get pulled into reacting and forgetting that babies operate with their own independent thoughts, feelings and motivations. Understanding your child's personality makes it easier to cope when your child's behaviour is really challenging. Did you know you can identify someone's temperament (how they respond to the world) from looking at early infant behaviour?

Babies display their own unique personality from the moment they are born. Some of their reactions are imprinted in their genes. These differences explain why some babies are actually harder to manage. This is amplified when you don't understand their style of communicating and expressing their needs.

When you find yourself reacting to your baby's cry, ask yourself what need is possibly being expressed at that moment – is he/she tired, hungry, bored, anxious, happy or playful? Make a time for observation, watch with curiosity and learn from what you see.

Here's a quick snapshot of observable traits to help you understand your baby, and to discover if they similar or not to you.

Activity levels

Babies show variation in their activity levels. Some seem happy to sit and watch the world go by while others are constantly moving and eager to stand up well before their little bodies can. This requirement impacts on play choices and routine.

You might relate to this trait if you are an on-the-go type of person who is energised by keeping busy. On the other hand, you may be someone who is happy to sit and read a book. Babies high in activity levels can be a shock to the system if it is the opposite of you. This type of baby moves quickly between activities, can resist sitting still, and appears fidgety when not given a chance to move. At the other end are the babies who are sitters and are happy to be strapped into a pram at the café as long as there are things to see. Knowing that activity preference is inbuilt helps us to accept that this will dictate the type of play preferences of the baby, and meeting those activity needs will pay off in their level of calmness.

Intensity levels

How loudly does your baby express its feeling – whether it be laughing, crying or somewhere in-between? Hunger, the feel of a wet nappy, and fatigue may be expressed to variable levels of intensity. The flip side to a baby who expresses itself with loud shrieks is that they often become assertive adults. How they respond to noise and touch influences how your child feels, too.

You will know fairly quickly if your child is intense by their reaction to times they don't get their own way. A delay to being fed when hungry or to being told no to something they want to do will be communicated with a loud outburst from the baby. The same goes for the times they are happy; they will show you enjoyment in a way that might seem dramatic if you are more quietly spoken. At least with high intensity you can't miss how they feel but you may need to coach them about how to express themselves for different situations – such as what is acceptable at a party compared to a classroom. If your child is particularly even tempered it doesn't mean they don't get bothered by things. It's just they show it in subtle ways such as looking away. You can tune into these subtle actions and help them put a name on what they are feeling to bolster their sense of what they like and dislike.

Frustration levels

Frustration levels sit alongside intensity and relate to the ability to continue with tasks when they get hard. This might show itself by the baby's response to being placed on their tummy or moving quickly between toys if they can't work out how to use it. It doesn't mean you have an "angry" baby but one that will benefit from learning to keep trying. They will respond to reassurance and support to build patience. Persistent learners might seem easier to manage and praise, but their desire for independence can get in the way of readily asking for help.

If your child seems to get easily frustrated it won't be hard to notice when they are upset but it might feel tiresome just how often they communicate this to you, and their lack of ability to wait when you have your hands full. Talking to them about why there is a delay and validating what is causing their frustration helps them to learn to cope and keep trying. It makes sense biologically to be like this as it ensures your needs are met. Children less prone to showing frustration usually spend more time alone as they seem so self-contained. They need the input just as much, and benefit from being offered support to cope with setbacks so they learn that asking for help is a good thing.

Adaptability

Adaptability is also something you're born with. At one end of the scale are babies that fall asleep anywhere, and at the other end there are babies who will only sleep in their cot at home at regular times. Kids, who don't handle changes to the routine, need extra time to prepare for what's coming up and some choice to restore some sense of control. In contrast the go-with the flow baby might seem like a dream but they risk being overlooked in times of a change that they aren't happy about.

Adaptable babies will declare themselves early by how easily they fit into your routine. They move easily between parents and are happy to go on holidays as they approach new situations with curiosity and respond quickly to changes in routines. They might require help to refrain from getting carried away and to know that it is okay not to like something. At the other end of the scale are children who react poorly to change. This is not all bad as they seek out routine and respond to it, which can make life less chaotic. They can be helped by you to ease into new activities and be reassured so they cope with change.

Sociability

Sociability is also inbuilt. While it can be enhanced and supported the reality is some of us are simply wired to be more social by nature. Some babies smile more easily, seek out eye contact with everyone and are happy to go to anyone. In contrast others are cautious and prefer to self-entertain. This can be tough if you are highly extroverted and don't understand why all the social exposure hasn't rubbed off on your baby. Social babies help parents feel as if they're doing a great job. All babies can learn to be social in their own way.

The sociable babies might seem easier, and in some ways they are, as they will respond positively to the opportunity to meet people, and will even relish the chance to go to the super market. Less naturally social babies get there in their own way and rely on you to help them transition – perhaps starting to meet others from the safety of your arms while seeing you smile and interact. Smaller groups and time to warm up usually brings out the best response and they can be just as smiley and interactive as their socialite counterparts in their own way …

Responding to your child with an informed parenting approach allows you to better support your child's needs.

We put a great deal of pressure on ourselves to be all that we can to our children. We must remember that not everything comes down to nurture over nature. Accepting your child's personality for what it is, allows room for finding creative ways to cater to their needs.

Now it's over to you:

- ➢ Watch your child play with an object; jot down some notes on where they sit on the list of the traits mentioned above.

- ➢ Likewise check in on your own state. Have you been attending to the PLEASE skills?

- ➢ Remember, old habits die hard. Sometimes we are trying to correct patterns that have been handed down over many generations.

> By working through this list you will move from seeing your child as self-centred and always screaming to getting to the heart of the reason they are behaving that way.

> Practise adopting a stance of curiosity and compassion.

It works with all other interpersonal relationships, too.

Case in Point

A 34 year old mother of three children presented for an interview to join a therapeutic play group to work on her goal of finding time to play with her youngest child. She said he was different to her first two children and was very demanding of her time. The first two babies had been easy going. They would sleep anywhere and entertained each other as they were only 15 months apart. She had anticipated that with a four-year gap that this baby was going to slot into the family routine and go with the flow too.

When it was suggested that we spend some time working out his unique personality and way of expressing himself she was dismissive and said defensively that wasn't her issue as he was her third child, and she had concluded he was stubborn and he needed to adjust. Exploration of her own childhood highlighted that she was raised in a strict household and she and her two sisters were obedient and very independent. She had not considered that her own past experiences and her first two babies were clouding her ability to see her son for who he was.

Once she had a handle on what parenting beliefs she carried she was able to see her son differently. She was asked to read a book to him and follow his lead. He pushed the book away and motioned to the floor. She reflected that he did like to be on the move and he let her know quite clearly what his needs were. Before the session she had used adult words such as stubborn and angry. She finished the sessions being able to describe his needs clearly.

To Recap

By now you are learning a great deal about yourself and how this plays out in your role as a parent. I often say to people that if you haven't explored the impact of your childhood on the type of parent you are or made peace with how you were parented, you will no doubt find yourself repeating patterns, actively avoiding them, feeling challenged by seeing parts of yourself in your child, or hearing your own parents in your parenting.

Your Task

Your challenge is to remember to practice what you have learnt. Actively tune into your child and ask yourself what are they trying to tell you.

Check to see if you are operating from an unhelpful childhood pattern, and ask yourself how you would like to respond next time.

Knowledge is power. Knowing how you and your child have similar and different personalities promotes understanding.

Next

In the next chapter you will learn how to name your emotions, what they are trying to tell you, and how to make sense of them and manage them more effectively.

Part 3
Manage Your Emotions And Thoughts

Calm is so much better than chaos

Chapter 7

Manage Your Emotions

That's the way to tame them

PARENTING can be a huge shake up to your emotional system. Often this shakeup occurs as soon as your baby is born. The emotional connection you immediately feel towards your new baby is countered by your concern that you might not be a good enough mother. If your emotions are in conflict, this creates pressure.

Being able to name our emotions and pinpoint the triggers for them is, in essence, what we need to be able to do to take charge of managing emotions. Psychologist and mindfulness expert Dan Siegel is famous for saying "if you can name it you can tame it" as you create some distance and see the emotion instead of being in it where there is no control.[16]

Let's start by defining what an emotion is. In its simplest form it is sensation that is felt somewhere in the body.[17] Emotions communicate to our brains through different body sensations. Each emotion feels different and is individual.

Figuring out what exactly you are feeling and why can be complicated. Yet it is an important skill to be able to accurately interpret how you feel, and also to be able to express yourself clearly to others.

Let's look at a common example of where anger is triggered in parenting. Your child is hanging over a high balcony or standing in the middle of a busy street. From a safety perspective it makes sense that your first response is to yell to get their attention, thus attempting to protect them from harm. Your next response will be influenced by what body sensations you feel and your own childhood experiences. You are likely to experience tension, elevated heart rate and quickened breathing as your body prepares to respond to the threat. If you respond angrily to your child's behaviour this is an unconscious learned behaviour. When we do this, we are letting anger cloud the deeper fear response. Connecting with fear will allow you to move towards engaging with your child and showing them how much you love them and that you were worried about their safety. When you eventually calm down from anger, you may feel shame about your angry response and that's why identifying fear allows you to express yourself more clearly.

Another common emotion felt by parents is anxiety. It is almost always about fear of something or someone being a threat – whether it is real or imagined. Thoughts of not being good enough or worrying something bad is going to happen can set off anxiety reactions. New mums often express their worries about keeping their baby safe from harm or question if they are doing a good enough job as a mum. Tapping into the fear driving the anxiety (felt as muscle tension, heart and breath racing) and expressing it out loud, takes away its power. You can then do something about it. You may not be able to remove the situation driving your anxiety but you can do something to reduce the anxiety intensity.

Distraction is a really useful way to take a break from your worries. Any activity can be used to refocus on something else.

Anxiety is also really sensitive to changes in breathing. Getting good at breathing from your stomach for a longer deeper breath is one of most powerful things you can do to stop anxiety in its tracks. We don't think about our breathing very often, at least not until we feel stressed and it becomes harder to breathe freely. Getting into the habit of practicing breathing when you feel calm sets you up with a skill you can call on when you experience a strong emotion.

The good news is that by practicing naming your emotions you can get better at recognising your feelings and what the emotion is trying to tell you. Once it is processed and understood, the intensity dials down so you can get on with enjoying your life. A researcher from UCLA had one group of people who were scared of spiders to label the anxiety they felt when near a spider. The results showed that the group who actively named their fear had significantly lower physical arousal levels and were able to get close to the spider. The results supported the theory that when you become clearer about your fear, it can help you to better regulate it.[18] Spiders and babies – who knew there was a link!

Let's look at a range of well-known emotions, what body sensations are associated with each, and what they do for you. Once you understand what the emotion is trying to tell you, it won't feel so overwhelming. You will see in the table how emotions differ in terms of body sensations and what they are trying to tell us. You may not agree exactly with the descriptions but use the information to inform you how your body tells you what it is feeling.

Remember that we don't feel emotions in our brain: we feel them in our body.

It takes practice to tune into your body and move away from operating on autopilot.

Common Emotions (other names for the emotion)	Body Sensations	Function of Emotion
Sadness also felt as grief, disappointment, sorrow, hopelessness	Heavy limbs, tight chest, teary, sunken posture	Loss of something or someone; telling us to seek comfort
Joy also pleasantness, happiness, contentedness, satisfaction, relaxedness	Lowered heart rate and breathing rate, relaxed posture, smile	Feel pleasure from something or someone
Anxiety also as fear, tension, scared, worried	Increased heart rate, hard to breath, shaking, tense body, restlessness	Keep us safe from danger or set off by a worry
Anger can be rage, impatience, frustration, upset	Increased heart rate, hot, clench jaws and fists	Motivate us to act to correct a block to a goal

Common Emotions (other names for the emotion)	Body Sensations	Function of Emotion
Guilt also sense of failure, uncomfortableness, feeling bad	Tight chest, forehead creased, downcast gaze	Acting outside of the values or behaviour you find acceptable

How many different emotions can you name?

Let's think of a few: happy; sad, angry, surprised, frightened, sick, guilty, envious, bored, puzzled, curious, tired. (Can you add to the list?)

Where do you feel emotions most strongly in your body? In your chest, stomach, legs.

Perhaps you are not even aware of the link between what you feel in your body and what it is trying to tell you about how you feel. Drawing on the some of the ideas in the table above should help you see the connection between different sensations.

When you make the link between body sensation and emotion, you realise that the way to change how you feel is through making sense of unpleasant sensations.

To help you tune into how your body conveys to you what emotion you are feeling, consider a strong emotion you experience often. What are the sensations you feel in your body? Here is an example to get you started …

Imagine you are racing through your morning routine of tightly executed actions to get your baby to day care and yourself to a morning meeting on time. Let's dial up the stress by adding that you are giving a presentation for the first time since you returned from maternity leave. You find yourself in unexpected road works and there is nothing you can do to change the situation. Immediately you feel hot, notice your heart rate and breath rate quicken. You grip the steering wheel and feel tightening in your neck and shoulders. This is your body telling you how anxious and frustrated it feels about the blockage in the way of your being on time. Intensity is heightened as you are flooded with negative thoughts about the fact you *should* have left earlier, people will be *judging* you for not being committed enough to the job since you had a family, and *fearing* your job is in jeopardy. All this happens inside of you within a minute of seeing the road closure sign.

Being able to breathe steadily is a critical skill to halting stress and emotion intensity. A really simple technique is the breathing exercise wherein you count your breaths on your fingers according to the following method:

> ➢ Tune into your breath by focusing on the physical sensation of your breath passing in and out of your nose.

> ➢ Notice that the air temperature is slightly cooler on the way in compared to the way out.

> ➢ Pay attention to your stomach and its rise and fall (like a balloon inflating and deflating) with each breath cycle.

➢ Count to 3 breathing in; hold for 3 counts; breath out for count of 3 (breath out for longer if you can and you'll feel even calmer).

➢ Now complete 5 cycles of breathing, keeping track by using your index finger to run up and down each finger on the opposite hand.

In the intense emotion scenario there is a chance that just by changing your breathing rate and depth, you can tell your body not to freak out. As the brain is flooded with oxygen you can think more logically. You can now see there are options such as you might still make it on time or you could make a phone call and ask for your presentation to be moved to later in the agenda.

Our body's sensory systems (there are 5 senses – sight, hearing, smell, touch, vision) are taken in through the environment, and powerful movement sensors (inside the body) can be used to help us feel calmer.[19] You can literally turn down the emotion intensity knob by soothing stress levels through the senses. Once you feel calmer, you can take action to deal with the situation at hand.

Sense of Touch is felt as a light brush against your skin or on a deeper level from a massage or by being under a heavy blanket. This has a powerful effect on the body and can lower your heart rate. Your breathing slows and sends calming messages to the brain. Examples include deep massage, a firm hug, wearing comfortable clothes, going bare feet, fiddling with something.

Sense of Smell is powerful and is a quick pathway to calm because it has close links to the emotion centre of the brain – the limbic system. Smells are taken in through the nose as odours, and many can be detected at once. Smells can prompt memories and also alert us to danger. Knowing what smells you find pleasant can be harnessed and used when you need a quick stress release. Examples include the smell of fresh cut grass has been found to elicit joyful and relaxed feelings. The sense of smell is linked to taste – sometimes when you have a cold you lose your sense of smell and that can come with a loss of taste. Taking the time to savour the smell of a meal or a fragrance can add to your sense of calm. Examples include aromatherapy, fresh air, lavender, flowers, perfumes, candles.

Sense of Taste (eating includes bite, chew, suck, texture, temperature) – the sense combines taste receptors in your tongue with powerful sensors in your jaw that are activated when chewing. Chewing alone can help us to feel calm which is why extra chewy foods can be calming. Examples include chewing gum, crunchy food, herbal tea, lollipops.

Sense of Vision is the information taken in through our eyes and is the primary way that we see what is going on around us. It can also be used when you recall pleasant images or memories as a way to feel calm. We all vary with how much light and type of visual stimuli is calming to us. For some, turning down the lights is calming, and for others being out on a bright sunny day is uplifting. Knowing what you like to look at allows you to seek out those images or recall them when you want to feel calm. Examples include changing the lighting, wearing sunglasses, seeing pleasant images, watching a sunrise, seeing waves crashing, watching bubbles or fish swimming in a tank, scrolling social media feed, or undertaking a word search.

Sense of Hearing is a more active sense then you think. Sound waves travel through the ear canal as vibrations and are involved with our sense of balance. Individuals find different sounds calming – from complete silence, to nature sounds, to certain types of music such as classical through to heavy metal. When you hear your favourite sounds your whole body relaxes, blood pressure drops and muscle tension eases. The same is true for unpleasant sounds, such as screaming kids. The noise is felt through the whole body as tension. So the next time you react strongly to sound know that what you hear has a strong influence on how you feel. Examples include music, silence, podcasts, white noise, and so on.

Sense of Movement is detected in our joints and muscles and is the most powerful way for the body to induce calm. The body craves to move when we are still for too long. It needs to release tension. It's why we often change our posture when we sit for too long. We don't need vigorous movements to ease the body's tension. Sometimes it comes out as a natural movement – by rocking, or tapping a foot, and can progress to getting up and walking around the room. Our sense of movement works together with the inner ear, which is responsible for our sense of balance, telling us where our body is in space each time we move. Moving the body about to varying levels of speed can be just what it needs to feel calm. Examples include intense exercise, gentle stretching, walking, swinging in a hammock, lifting weights.

Here is an example of a self soothing with the senses plan that can be written up and used to remind you of your favourite sensations to try when you feel stressed out:

Touch – deep massage, a hug, comfortable clothes, bare feet.

Smell – aromatherapy, fresh air

Taste – chew gum, crunchy food, herbal tea

Vision – change lighting, sunglasses, pleasant images

Hearing – music, silence, podcast

Movement – intense exercise, gentle stretching, walking

Case in Point

On maternity leave from her job as an immigration lawyer, this 40 year old mother of a three month old baby presented as feeling overwhelmed by anxiety and had recently developed severe lower back pain due to not being able to put her baby down all day. She hardly slept at night even when her baby was sleeping. She reported not coping with the sound of her baby's cry – hence she held the baby to keep her quiet.

Counselling involved helping her see that she felt anxious in response to her baby. She named her emotions as fearful and panicked. She reported strong body sensations of anxiety – racing heart rate, breathing difficulty, muscle tension that ran down her back, no appetite, and unable to sit down due to her baby crying and leg restlessness.

It was explained that the function of anxiety is to keep us safe. Mums often feel anxious when caring for their baby. Anxiety is the brain's survival response to changes in body sensations – such as fast/restricted breathing sets off the fight or flight response. However, as mothers feeling anxious we don't stop to consider if we are actually in danger. It is important to be able to escape from real danger, of course, but it is important to know this part of the brain doesn't stop to check before leaping into a response to the body sensations we are feeling. This anxiety is also fueled by thoughts of the past when the baby cried or previous stressful events where anxiety was reinforced.

She was provided with breathing instruction to inhibit the brain response. She was advised that when breathing deepens, in particular the out-breath, to a count of 6, it sends the brain a message that you are safe.

Her blind spots were that her career had reinforced her need for perfectionism, order and control which had led to misinformation about babies crying. She was advised to look at how her anxious state influenced how she handled her baby's cries.

She was observed playing with her baby on the ground and instructed on how to regulate her own breath and to offer the baby different things to look at to distract baby from being aware of not being held. Once she saw that it was not doing harm for the baby to vocalise distress and that she could change a play item or position, she increased her confidence to leave the baby more on play mat or in the rocker, pram and crib. By setting up a more manageable daily routine with her baby, she had time to do other things such as have a shower, do chores and even do things for herself that she found relaxing such has streaming through social media. With balance restored, her self-reported anxiety levels dropped considerably.

To Recap

Being able to name our emotions and pinpoint the triggers for them is, in essence, what we need to be able to do to take charge of managing emotions. Figuring out what exactly you are feeling and why can be complicated. Yet it is an important skill to be able to accurately interpret how you feel, and also to be able to express yourself clearly to others. Learn to name emotions by connecting body sensations and function of different emotions. Adopt calming strategies such as deep breathing and sooth through your senses to reduce intensity.

Your Task

Design your own calming tool box. Practise the calming breathing exercise.

Next

In the next chapter you will learn what thoughts have to do with why we feel emotions in varying levels of intensity.

Chapter 8

Control Your Thoughts And Emotions Differently

You CAN cope with your child's tantrums

SOMETIMES our reactions can be overwhelming simply because we didn't stop to check if our response is backed up with the facts. Maybe our reaction has been caused by an automatic response to the thoughts sparked each time we experience the same event.

Here's an example – your baby is crying ceaselessly it seems. You react by feeling stressed. And before long you are an absolute wreck. Stop for a moment. Remember that crying is a baby's primary means of communication. Consider why your baby is crying – maybe it needs comfort, a nappy change, feeding, and so on, or it might be in pain. Armed with the facts you can take the appropriate action. The baby stops crying. Your stress levels abate and you are on your journey to calm.

Our minds are like hard drives and don't naturally pause and consider if the thought is serving us well. Without any introspection that means our minds have already decided how we will respond before we are even conscious of it. To understand this, think about the times your brain responds on instinct – such as when a baby reaches out towards a hot cup of coffee and you intervene reflexively, grabbing the coffee and moving it away, afterwards thinking "wow that was close". Similarly if you stop your pram on a hill and forget to clamp the brake, you act super-fast and without thinking to grab the pram.

Being able to respond quickly to danger is essential when raising a small child who has no sense of safety. This very basic survival-end of the brain is quick but not always logical and can respond to past memories and fearful thoughts that don't require a fight or flight response. The deeper part of the brain doesn't stop to consider if the threat is real or imagined. Its sole function is to keep us and the people around us safe. Afterwards the rational part of the brain comes in. It communicates with the other parts to decide whether it will allow you to relax or not.

To enlarge on this point – the stress response (flight or fight) centre of the brain can cause us to overreact in a stressful situation when there is actually not an imminent danger. You no doubt can readily recognise those situations where you've jumped in boots and all. Maybe it was when you were frightened and you blurted out something that you later deeply regretted. Or perhaps when your child was doing something that could be dangerous, you yelled frantically and swore at him. Psychologist Daniel Goleman discovered that you can prevent or stop this "survival" response, thanks to a delay of approximately six seconds between the stress response centre of the brain and the rational part of the brain kicking in. In those six seconds you can try focusing on a pleasant image, and breathe deeply. This way you gain control over the fight or flight response and you can choose a more appropriate way to react to the situation.[20]

Other ways of turning your mind to logical thinking in a

stressful situation that is not as dire as you originally thought might include counting backwards from 100 in sevens, or naming fruits starting with the first six letters of the alphabet – anything that can create a pause and allow time for your more rational self to activate. Now that you have awareness of the brain's two different response times to stressful situations, you can practise calming your emotions when exposed to your triggers. You have created a button that can be pushed in times when there is actually no imminent danger. Don't forget that the reactions we have to stress can be our old emotional patterns trying to play themselves out. By mastering our reactions we're progressing well on our journey to calm.

We have roughly 50.000 thoughts a day with some people having as few as 12,000 and others as many as 60,000. An extensive study found approximately 95% of thoughts are repetitive, with approximately 80% being negative thoughts.[21]

It's worth reviewing how you think. It's a way of getting a stronger handle on how and why you react the way you do. Just as with any new skill, changing years of thinking a certain way will take a fair bit of practice. To see results you need to put the time in.

If you are like most people, you will find that you have a lot more negative thoughts than positive ones. We also tend to remember and feel the impact of negative events more strongly than positive ones. This is worth bearing in mind as you journey into motherhood because you might feel alarmed by just how much of your attention goes into the less pleasant parts of the day. Just as we need to be able to respond quickly to danger, this over emphasis on negative events is also a survival mechanism built into the brain from caveman days when they endured real threats all the time. So the tendency to dwell on the negative rather than the positive aspects of the day is instinctive.

The next time you perceive that you had a really tough day perhaps think about the truth of it. Maybe something did go wrong – such as your child refusing to have its morning nap. You can reduce the impact of the negativity by paying closer attention to your thoughts throughout the day. Catch yourself stuck in negative thinking or pay close attention to moments you feel good. The brain is malleable towards more optimistic thinking. Another way of getting off of the negativity roundabout is to get into the habit of naming what you are grateful for. Start simple like the hot shower, fresh coffee, a smile.

Think about a strong feeling you have associated with a parenting stressor that you would like to change. Perhaps it is one of these scenarios:

- ➢ Guilt about not spending enough quality time with your child after a long day at work
- ➢ Anxiety about whether you'll ever sleep through the night again (after another night of little sleep)
- ➢ Frustration with how you handled a tantrum from someone a fraction of your age.

Let's review what evidence there is to justify the situation of responding angrily to a toddler tantrum. Consider you are a scientist for a moment. Start by unpacking where the anger comes from by noticing your automatic negative thoughts which are part of our early conditioning and can dominate how you think and respond.²² What assumptions, interpretations or black and white thinking might be influencing you to feel so frustrated?

Assumptions are rules you carry that you learnt in childhood such as "children should respect their elders". Do you take on the mantra of "I need to yell to be heard" or "Nothing else works when they are crying loudly" or "Tantrums are rude behaviour and it's my job to teach them to behave"? There are many more examples and they all reinforce it being okay to react with anger. It's probably something you carried over from your childhood.

Interpretations are the meaning we give to a situation such as "Why couldn't they just tell me what they wanted?"

Black and white thinking is defined as those extreme thoughts such as "Yelling is so bad" and "I am a horrible parent".

You can see from the points above that the feelings barometer is directly influenced by the automatic belief system. Add in your values, past experiences and underlying rules of how we believe life should be, and you can find plenty of fodder to feed your reaction.

Now comes the contradiction. Consider that developmentally toddlers don't have the self-regulation skills to be calm all the time. By reacting to a tantrum the way we do (as listed above) we are actually role modelling the opposite behaviour of what we want, when the child could actually be in genuine pain or trying to communicate a need in the best way it can.

> ➢ Ask yourself if your values are supporting the methods you're using.

- Check if whether feeling angry fits with the available evidence. You might find yourself reconsidering your reaction.
- Get into the habit of observing your thoughts, providing space to review and reframe unhelpful thoughts.
- Reframe your thoughts this way perhaps – "My child is doing his/her best to tell me how he feels".

This shift in your approach will help you find a level of calm to better manage a tantrum.

Don't expect this strategy to work the first time you try it – it does take practice. If there is a pattern of tantrums or some other challenging behaviour that you find yourself easily bothered by, it is highly likely that you will need to practise stopping and noticing your interpretations over and over. Sometimes we need to step away to regroup.

An important rule of first aid is to check your own safety before rendering assistance to others. It's the same in parenting – to be an effective parent you need to attend to your own stress level before turning to manage your child's challenging behaviour.

Another way to practice this skill is to brainstorm on paper your thoughts for and against responding in different ways. You will start to see how influential your mind is in determining the action you take …

Try reflecting on a stressful event and what automatic negative thoughts come up. Then see how they drove how you felt in that moment. When you dig a little, rarely do strong emotions exist without affirming thoughts.

Ask yourself if acting that way was really effective?

Revisiting our interpretations when we are calm allows us to see the situation through a cleaner lens. With practice we can change our emotions by getting into the habit of checking facts.[23] Stop leaving your thoughts unsupervised as they will end up dictating how you feel without you even knowing.

Case in Point

A 35 year old first time mother of a six month old baby presented feeling depressed and not enjoying being a mum. She was perplexed as she thought she had ticked all the boxes for a happy life – own home, happy relationship, successful career as a nurse and now a healthy baby. She had completed three years of fertility treatment to conceive her precious child and she wasn't content. She said she blamed herself for not being able to fall pregnant and the cost of treatment had been difficult financially. When asked how she was going as a mum she said she doubted her ability to know what her baby wanted. She was particularly bothered by her baby not sleeping through the night as she knew all the tricks to sleep settling and yet her child woke every two hours. It was apparent early on that she talked about herself in a critical way. This was not just about the baby but that she was a hopeless friend who never returned calls and she felt lazy not to have returned to exercising. When asked if she thought she'd speak to a friend the way she does herself she conceded that she would probably be more understanding but that pushing herself had helped her in the past achieve her goals.

She was encouraged to consider how accurate her automatic thoughts were compared to reality. She had not considered that her work as a nurse was shaping her to feel frustration with her baby. She was bothered that her baby did not always respond to the clockwork routine where sleep times were scheduled. At work she was efficient and organised and she often received feedback from patients about how caring she was. Fatigue also increased her propensity towards critical thinking. When she was asked to keep a record of her baby's sleep, some nights the baby woke only once a night and yet in the mother's mind it was a different story. She was responsive to education re black and white thinking and was agreeable to keeping a thought diary. Just by writing her thoughts down helped her develop a different perspective on her thoughts. She understood that babies are unpredictable and that having a routine was serving her well, it just wasn't reinforced like it is at work ...

To Recap

Our thoughts are not necessarily based on actual facts. It causes us stress when we react to those thoughts in ways that are not what we wanted to do as a parent. Often we're perpetuating behaviours our parents used in rearing us. We need to re-programme our thoughts to take control of what we think. For example we could stop and think that a toddler's temper tantrum is not merely bad behaviour but is actually the child showing frustration at his inability to communicate what he wants.

Your Task

Keep a record for a day of your thoughts – the ones that repeat, stand out, bother you, and please you. Then audit them for being factual. Ask yourself are they true or false.

Next

In the next chapter you will learn what you can do to deal with situations that have been fact-checked as true and yet have left you feeling stressed.

Chapter 9

Problem Solving Relieves Stress

Maybe yelling isn't the answer!

HAVE you identified any parenting behaviours you want to change? Perhaps reading the earlier chapters has sparked your awareness of something in your parenting style that bothers you. Have you noticed that it's nearly impossible to change habits by telling yourself to do things differently? To make changes you have to look at the reasons you have those behaviours in the first place. For example, yelling at your offspring or at others when you are under stress from your baby is a common happening for parents. Resolving the issue is closely tied to becoming a calm parent. It is probably times when your child is not listening to you and you are time-pressured that are the hardest times to resist the urge to repeat the problem behaviour.

Assume you wanted to shift from yelling to using a kind soft voice with your child. The first step to change is to understand the pros and cons attached to the action of yelling.

People vary in their response to not being able to solve a problem. It can cause panic and frustration for some and an opportunity to work on a weakness for another. The difference is whether they have developed this important life skill. Stress will continue until the problem is solved. Teaching children to apply a step-by-step process to times they won't get their own way has been found to lower family stress levels and to reduce children's behavioural problems and of going on to develop more serious issues.[24]

The Pros and Cons of Yelling:

The Pros – it gets results; it's a physical relief to yell

The Cons – it doesn't yield lasting results; it scares your child; it's not how you want to role model.

Another example of a parenting behaviour you might want to change is being a soft touch. Do you often cave-in to demands to avoid conflict? Do you say yes to more screen time, sweets, sleeping in your bed, milk in the middle of the night and so on?

The Pros and Cons of Saying YES Instead of NO:

The Pros – instant relief; the child feels good; they tell you they love you.

The Cons – reinforcing the child's expectation it will get whatever it wants; there is more resistance when you say no.

It can be quite overwhelming to see yourself repeating a behaviour you don't want to do, and it can leave you feeling hopeless and helpless to change it. Consider what you stand to gain by resisting the urge. This should give you the motivation to pause and consider what you've learnt about soothing your emotions, fact checking, and thinking about why you are currently reacting as you are. When you do this, you are being a good problem-solver.

This book is all about teaching you that you can change parts of yourself.

The Steps to Working on Behaviour Change

- ➢ Identify a problem behaviour
- ➢ Consider the pros and cons
- ➢ Make a commitment to change
- ➢ Decide what you can do to regulate emotions and thoughts to support your parenting goal

It's a good idea to start small and build your confidence. For example, maybe you have a young baby and avoid play time because it feels unproductive. Simply add in 5 minutes of mat time, or read a board book after a feed. Another example – an older baby might want to feeds itself but makes a terrible mess, making you want to feed your baby. Resist the urge!

Over to You

- ➢ Think of a behaviour you want to change, record a list of pros and cons for stopping the behaviour. This little piece of paper becomes your cheat sheet to refer to and motivate you.

- ➢ Decide what will be your replacement behaviour – such as you might try to whisper or name the distress that you see each time you have the urge to yell. Or give choices/reasons why you should say no instead of always saying yes.

- ➢ After a few days, evaluate how you've gone. Has the frequency or intensity dropped off? Is there a pattern to when you slip up? Perhaps you've slipped up when you haven't attended to any of the PLEASE skills, or you haven't spoken to an adult all day. It might help to keep a record. This can be recorded directly into your phone or on a pad beside the bed each night.

Problem-solving skills can also be applied to a specific problem in your life. These skills can be applied to almost any problem scenario when you are at a crossroad or you feel stuck in a situation. Start by considering what that confusion is about. Beneath the problem there are always solutions. You just mightn't like the options available. Situations such as needing to leave a relationship or quit job that isn't family-friendly will cost you security but will pay off in the long run.

Brainstorming possible solutions on your own or with someone else might lead to the surprise discovery that you do have options. You can literally move from feeling stuck, to having a sense of hope that there is way through – even if you don't like everything about your options.

Given that parenting is a long-haul commitment; building good problem-solving skills is an important tool to develop.

Often from the moment they are pregnant and accelerating after they give birth, mothers worry about so many things …

> ➢ Am I doing a good enough job? How do I ensure my baby gets enough sleep?
>
> ➢ Is my baby eating a balanced diet?
>
> ➢ What can I do to deal with tantrums? Or stop my child from being so clingy?
>
> ➢ Is my child making friends, doing well at school?
>
> ➢ Should I return to work?
>
> ➢ And the list goes on …

With so much information available through the internet, social media and also advice from family and friends, it is easy to feel confused and overwhelmed.

I suggest that you deal with the identified problem by brainstorming possible solutions. Consider every option that comes to mind, even the silly ones. Be creative. Then look at the pros and cons for each solution identified. This allows you visualise the factors you are weighing up. It will also highlight what factors you value most.

All parenting dilemmas have an emotional impact on you and this adds to the pressure.

Let's explore together a common scenario of whether or not you return to work. Your options are yes; no; to work full time; to work part-time; to work flexible hours; to job share; to work from home.

Working from home is trending more and more these days, although some women find domesticity distracts them from their job. These days some family-friendly employers encourage employees to bring their children to work where nurseries are set up. It's a great option for women (who are giving birth later in life) who don't want to lose career momentum by taking prolonged maternity leave ...

The Pros and Cons of Returning to Work

The Pros – financial benefits; regaining your sense of identity; improved self-esteem; greater social connection; a work-life balance; and lifestyle factors.

The Cons – the implications and cost of child care; less time for domestic matter; loss of quality time with your child; wasted time travelling; additional stresses attached to working.

There is often a compromise to reach on the other side of a good brainstorm session. Maybe you decide to find a job with fewer hours, or closer to home, or you arrange to share care with your partner, or you decide to wait until your child is older.

The Pros and Cons of Moving to a Bigger House

The Pros – more living space, a back yard, satisfaction of achieving a goal, less stress with more space for everyone's needs, more space to entertain family and friends.

The Cons – bigger mortgage and stamp duty costs, having to cut back on other living expenses, the stress of a move, the difficulty of finding the right place to buy, having to acquaint yourself with a new neighbourhood, unsure if you'll be any happier

As you can see there are often many points to weigh up on both sides. You might like to give each point a value rating of importance. Perhaps it opens up other options such as completing a small renovation on your existing home. If you do go ahead you'll need to make peace with all the cons such as a new budget, putting in the leg work to carry out your plan to find your dream home. On the other hand, if you stay you may see other financial benefits to not moving – such as more holidays, and finding novel ways of making your living space work.

Sometimes you might have to repeat the process a few times if your first choice doesn't work out.

It is important to evaluate your solution and to modify the plan if it doesn't yield the results you wanted. It is easy to give up on problem-solving at this point. When you do this, you remain stuck. Take a break and come back with a fresh mind.

Once all the issues are on the table, it is easier to decide the best way forward. Even issues such as how to budget for unexpected debts, or a change in health status can benefit from problem solving.

Try not to be pulled into the dark side of enduring a situation you can't change in that moment. Accept even the most challenging situations (that you once would never have chosen to face), and free-up space in your mind to problem solve.

Children respond to seeing the adults around them coping with stress by taking proactive action. We are their biggest influencers; there is nothing more powerful than showing not telling.

Once you get a handle on your own problem-solving, you can teach your kids how to turn their problems into solutions. There are loads of opportunities in play to assist them to find solutions when they get stuck, they can't do something or they are in a risky situation.

Toddlers are notorious for feeling frustrated when they can't do something and are pushing the limits of their new found physicality. Perhaps they love to climb on everything and you worry they will fall and hurt themselves. Help them find ways to extend themselves physically by taking them to the park and setting up safe things to climb on.

Siblings often fight when the younger one plays with the things of the elder child. They fear the younger child will damage the possession. Instead of being drawn into the argument, help them problem solve by looking at where they can store precious items that are not to be touched, and help the siblings decide what they can do together that will be fun.

Case in Point

A 30 year old mother of two children reported feeling stuck in an unhappy relationship where she had chosen to have a second child a year before because she didn't want to raise an only child. On the one hand she wanted her children to be raised in an intact family unit where they could afford private education for the children. On the other hand, she didn't want to remain in a relationship with her partner of five years who she had begun to resent. She said they had a newly mortgaged home and she didn't like his parenting style and would not want the children to spend time with him or be without her young children in her care full time.

Counselling involved providing space for her to tell her story and develop her awareness of what had drew her to this relationship was connected to the parenting she had received (her father had disrespected her mother and they had stayed together unhappily). She knew she had thoughts of leaving her husband, and their fighting in front of the children was affecting them. She reflected that her three year old son often mimicked his dad and talked back to her, which made her feel angry and set off the urge to walk out – although she never did.

She was responsive to a problem-solver approach to looking at the pros and cons of leaving. She was encouraged to seek legal advice regarding her financial settlement rights, and also advised that it would not be the end of the world to return to work. She agreed that her parents would likely help her if she was able to swallow her pride and tell them she was not happy in her marriage. To her surprise she had let her assumptions get in the way of reality. Through family mediation they reached a settlement and while it was financially hard and involved accepting that her children needed to see their father, they were better parents apart. She was also able to see that fear of judgement from others was not as bad as she had feared and her close friends told her they were proud of her making such a courageous decision. This was not a quick outcome and was processed over months. At the start of the process she accepted staying with her partner, albeit with her eyes open to the issue, while she laid the foundation for the split at a time when she felt completely able to cope with it.

To Recap

Good problem-solving skills turn problems into possible solutions. Whether it's deciding to return to work, or whether you should be saying no instead of yes, or how to curb your yelling, or any of the many problems that arise during parenting, look at the pros and cons of changing behaviour to help you address unhelpful patterns or to be better able to make difficult decisions.

Your Task

Grab a piece of paper and brainstorm the pros and cons attached to a problem you have with a parenting behaviour, or maybe a difficult decision you need to make.

Next

In the next chapter you will learn how to stand up for yourself to get your needs better met, and to give feedback successfully.

Chapter 10

Stand Up For Yourself

You're not anyone's dishcloth!

IT isn't always easy to ask for what you want, to give feedback when someone upsets you, or to say no to a request.

Being able to communicate your needs effectively is an important skill that will help you maintain all relationships in your life.

The #MeToo movement highlighted the fact than women don't always feel comfortable pushing back when their boundaries are overstepped. Among the reasons is that women worry they will sound rude – or they might fear they have misinterpreted the situation.

Do you get caught up in worrying about how other people perceive you? Are you afraid of saying "no" to helping someone out? (You might have a fear of being seen as selfish and that it is wrong to put yourself first). Perhaps you are judged as aggressive by someone you told off for being rude – or as a pushover if you avert your gaze and say nothing. In reality we can't control what others think of us.

There is oodles of research to show that learning to be more assertive with practice and changing the way you think not only increases your self-worth and relationship satisfaction but also lowers symptoms of depression and anxiety.

Now is your chance to review your boundaries and make a choice to focus on what is in your control. It doesn't always feel like it but we do ultimately choose what we say or don't say. The same goes for the effort you put in to reviewing your opinions that dictate how easy it is to express your needs and ask for help.

Cast your mind back to what sort of friendships you had at school. Did you have a large circle of friends, move friendship groups when conflict arose, put all your energy into one important friendship or feel like you didn't fit in and couldn't wait to leave? Given that we know that essentially our personalities don't change, it is useful to consider how you operate socially. This will allow you to play to your strengths. For example, if you know you struggle with transitions or you are highly sociable and struggle with alone time you will express yourself differently. Ideally while growing up, we are supported by our parents and other influential adults who help us navigate social skills, building confidence to stand up for our individual needs. If we learnt early to express ourselves and it was met positively, it will be an easier transition to identifying what our needs are as parents.

We can all benefit from fine tuning our assertiveness muscle. The solution might be in learning to respond with humour, or preparing kind words to use when you feel uncomfortable with the way another person is behaving towards you.

You have already become more familiar with your interpersonal style – whether you are a more direct straight-shooter or you are up the people-pleaser end of the continuum. Getting a handle on assertiveness just became a great deal more important now that you are a parent.

Remember that your reactions are the key to shaping your baby into someone fit for the world.

Even though we know we can't control other people's thoughts, why is it so hard to drive in your own lane without worrying about what others are thinking about you? It is in our biology to want to connect to and be accepted by the herd. This survivalist pull must be disarmed. Putting ourselves first moves us from survival to thrive mode. Like learning any skill, communicating assertively takes a great deal of practice.

Being able to communicate effectively is sure to be tested in your mum role. It will impact on how comfortable you are to discipline your child and to navigate conflict.

In fact, all the people in the relationships around you who support you and challenge you as a parent will on occasion need to be told how you feel. Take your partner for example. Perhaps you checked off your parenting rules before you decided to have kids, and went into the journey expecting you are still on the same page. Opinions change as we've already established; our own childhood blueprint is activated. It is unrealistic to expect that you both will parent the same way. You may wish to share this chapter and reach agreement about how you will check in on each other.

It is alarming how often people think it is okay to cast judgment on someone's parenting. From strangers at the supermarket to well-meaning loved ones, parenting opinions seem to be a free-for-all. It starts in pregnancy when people comment on your size for weeks of gestation and what you can and can't eat. How can someone else other than you possibly know why your baby is crying? They can't. I've known women to avoid the supermarket for this very reason.

The first step is to acknowledge, inside your head via self-talk, that you don't like what someone said to you. Try not to be critical that you didn't do anything about it. It doesn't always come naturally to give feedback. The roots to why you don't like giving feedback stems from your earliest role-models and your personality. When you look back at your childhood, were you shut down or encouraged to speak up?

Being heard early on, builds natural confidence in your ability to tell people when you feel upset or angry about their actions. Being able to stand up for yourself forms the base for building healthy relationships and getting your needs met long before you become a parent.

If you were to reflect on all the relationships around you, how often do you give feedback? Think about your partner, kids, friends, family, work and anyone you have contact with in your community. Do you find it easier to be honest to certain people and avoid others?

Pick someone you are (1) frustrated with; pinpoint what the trigger point was; or (2) you caved in and said yes when you wanted to say no.

Now have a conversation in your mind about what they did that bothered you or why you ignored your needs ahead of theirs. It can be a small thing that you would otherwise ignore. Minor points of conflict are often not addressed and then they grow into bigger misunderstandings.

Perhaps you hold assumptions as to why it is best to let it go. Whatever the reasons are that hold you back, most of the time we imagine a worse outcome than actually happens when you tell someone how you feel.

To get really good, practice these steps regularly in the mirror, or role play with someone:

> ➢ Tell the person how you feel and what your issue is using objective information. If you catch yourself making judgements, notice that. The last thing you want is a game of tennis (arguing back and forth). Feeling judged can ignite the calmest person to be on the defence.
>
> ➢ Consider the other person's perspective when delivering your feedback so it brings them onside.
>
> ➢ Suggest how it could be resolved.
>
> ➢ Name the benefits for the relationship (or for the other person) to bring you further to a resolution.
>
> ➢ Decide where your line is and whether the issue is worth persisting with if you hit a brick wall.

Practise this skill each day to help you get comfortable with giving feedback.

Be prepared for the possibility that it may not go to plan and you may need to hear the other party's' point of view and not like it. It is important to validate it even if you don't agree.

Negotiating an acceptable outcome may require you to be flexible on the best fit compromise.

Remember that you are only ever be 50% of any dynamic, and this means it isn't possible to resolve every issue.

Sometimes it helps to put yourself in the other person's shoes. You can do this by sitting in two different chairs or by just imagining in your head what you know about them and what they might be thinking that justifies their point of view. It is hard for the other person to maintain their defences when they hear you relay back what you have heard and what you wonder might be happening for them. Rarely do conflicts resolve with an attitude of "I am right" or with being unmovable on a viewpoint. Perhaps you haven't considered their arguments, and when you both take into account the others point of view you are more likely to reach a compromise than have a Mexican standoff.

Don't forget your skills in attending to hot-headed emotions where your mind tells you automatically what to think. These factors can cause a civil discussion to become an outright fight ...

If you can condition yourself into becoming an assertive communicator through regular practice, you're preparing yourself to give real-time feedback when you really need to. Your fear of confrontation comes from your past and doesn't exist in the present.

The more you practice giving feedback, the better your comfort level. While we can't control another person's reaction, we have a responsibility to ourselves to teach people how we want to be treated.

Getting it right is important modelling to our children. Don't forget to cheerlead yourself each time you give immediate feedback and watch how people treat you differently when they realise you won't put up with rudeness. Be prepared to walk away so they know you mean business.

Knowing how to express your needs clearly and objectively increases your chances of being heard and understood. Giving feedback and saying NO should not be feared – it is all in the delivery.

There is a common saying attached to parenting "monkey see: monkey do". You can guarantee your child is always your audience to how you communicate. They see how you interact with your partner, how you address disagreements with them, and even how you deal with those annoying random uninvited marketing phone calls.[25] You now have the most important reason to tweak your communication skills. Harness all that you have learnt and push through any discomfort as if you keep your feedback objective it is hard to refute.[26]

> **Case in Point**
>
> *This 30 year old mother had three children under five years old. Due to having three children in close succession, after the first child the mother stopped working so that she could care for her young children to avoid the high cost of child care. Her partner of ten years worked full-time in a high profile job that was stressful and often required long hours. He returned home each night expecting the house to be clean and dinner ready. Prior to having children they shared the domestic load and had similar jobs and earning capacity. Since having children he controlled the finances and questioned any transactions she had not discussed with him.*
>
> *Counselling involved helping her see that she had a right to equal say financially and that staying home with three children was hard work and something her partner didn't seem to appreciate what exactly is involved. She was advised to look at how her pleaser personality had led to her avoiding conflict. Role plays were conducted to consider ways she could respond more assertively when*

her partner criticised her, to negotiate collaborative financial control, and that it was more than okay to expect him to help out when he is at home.

She was encouraged to cheer lead herself by naming three things she had achieved each day for her family and to practise telling her husband how it made her feel when he judged her before checking how her day has been. We joked that a role swap for a week would be an effective intervention but not one he would ever agree to as his upbringing of being raised in a family where his father was the bread winner and his mother did not work had resurfaced only after they had kids. We completed one couple session, suggested as education for him to learn about how to support his wife's anxiety. The session provided a useful medium to share how they both felt and to brainstorm new ways of communicating with each other from a non-judgmental stance.

To Recap

It isn't always easy to ask for what you want, to give feedback when someone upsets you, or to say no to a request. Don't get caught up in worrying about how other people perceive you. We can all benefit from fine tuning our assertiveness muscle. Being able to communicate effectively will impact on how comfortable you are to discipline your child and navigate conflict, and will make you an effective role model to your child.

Your turn

Start by practicing giving feedback on someone you feel totally comfortable with. Start with safe topics such "I like your outfit" or "The dinner you cooked was delicious".

Next

In the next chapter you will bring all that you have learnt so far into action as you find out why all the hype about mindfulness and its relevance to calm parenting.

PART 4
TO BE CALM, LEARN TO BE PRESENT

Don't be on automatic pilot

Chapter 11

Be Tuned-in To Your Child

It's the way to calm

IF there is one thing that can make a big difference to how well you interact with your child and lead you on the pathway to calm, it is your capacity to pause and reflect before you respond. Call it mindfulness, aware parenting, being present, or being tuned-in – whatever you call it, it means you need to be present and not on auto pilot (something that's easy to do, given our busy lives) when you're parenting. Being able find that calm space in the heat of the moment is the penultimate skill to shifting from reacting to responding.[27]

Perhaps you have tried "mindfulness" because you've heard it's the answer to stress management. Perhaps you've tried apps, completed courses, and read other self-help books. Maybe you've even gone on a retreat and sat in silence for a week and, for a brief moment, felt the drop in your stress levels that the gurus rave about (only for your levels to lift up again once you were home).

What has happened is that you still have your old habits. Your mind never stops thinking; you don't feel any calmer. You're thinking about the past and the future (worrying about what has happened and what might happen), which is taking you out of the present moment. The reality is that all we have is the here and now. We get one go at life, so it is necessary to find achievable and functional ways to be tuned-in/switched-on/mindful in your parenting and other relationships.

Did you know that when you become involved in watching a funny video on youtube or enjoy eating a piece of high quality chocolate you are practicing mindfulness? Every time you do something with focused attention it turns down your thought machine and you become involved in the experience you are having, you are being mindful. You don't have to tuck yourself away in a dark room and chant *ohm* to find your mindful mojo.

Our individual needs are expressed through how we think, feel and behave. Likewise, our children have their own independent reactions and needs. At times it can feel as if your child is deliberately being difficult. That's not to say they can't detect times when you are feeling tired or distracted.

Being curious about and observing non judgmentally, what is going on for your child is a form of mindfulness.

Have a look at the two different ways the mother described below, interacts with her baby and see if you can pick the mindfulness approach:

"I can see you smiling, reaching for the rattle, making gurgling sounds. You must be happy." *versus* "I am noticing, not trying to change anything, just noticing you lying on the play mat, shaking the rattle. You have a smile on your face; you are making gurgling sounds. I'm your audience and smile back at you, enjoying this moment with you, holding myself in this moment by what I can see and hear".

"I can see you grimacing as you try to pull yourself up on the coffee table, you are angry that you don't have the strength to do it and that is silly as you are too young." *versus* "I am noticing you, but not trying to change anything, just noticing you attempt to pull yourself up on the coffee table. Your face is wrinkled; you vocalise and keep attempting to pull yourself up. I tell you I am here to help you, it is ok, let me help you stand up. Your face and demeanour changes once you are standing supported at the table".

Can you see the difference in each scenario?

You have an important role to care and influence but you can neither control the outcome of every scenario nor be to blame when things don't go to plan.

The key difference in the second response is adopting a non-judgmental stance. Taking the guesswork out allows you to focus on being present. Your mind will try and tell what it thinks is going on and what you *should* do. You might feel uncomfortable and notice a buildup of tension as you try to adopt this new approach. It will be hard at first to fight the urge to take action. All that we've learnt so far tells us that babies are their own unique selves. When we think we know what the baby is vocalising, we are often basing that opinion on our own bias. You might surprise yourself that, with practice, you start to see that judgments are not foolproof and can take you off course.

Let's look at some more examples of how being able to step back (being mindful) is a helpful skill to learn.

Everyone's been woken in the middle of the night by a crying baby. What's going on for baby? Are they deliberately trying to interrupt your sleep or have they woken due to hunger, a nightmare, transition to a new sleep routine, pain/sickness, and so on? It is our job to provide support to resettle them back to sleep. This is going to be hard to do if you are tired, up every night, feel ineffective with the strategies being used or feeling resentful. By being tuned-in to what your baby is trying to say allows you to respond from a place of calm.

When mums tell me they have just been to sleep school or had a sleep consultant out to the home to remedy the baby who doesn't sleep, they rarely say they were taught some miraculous new sleep cure. The objective eye of the professional reads the baby cues and points out blind spots that were reinforcing the baby's wakefulness. This supports the mother to be more mindfully armed with the confidence of knowing what works, and frees her from being weighed down with the emotion of not wanting to do anything that may harm her baby.

Similarly, when your children are fighting and you are trying to cook dinner, pause and ask yourself what is driving this scenario. Maybe they are tired and hungry. Are they seeking your attention? Did they have a bad day at child care or school? Siblings have a knack for knowing how to set each other off. If you can respond from a perspective of understanding, you will not only be more effective but you will also be modelling good coping skills. This helps them learn how to deal with big emotions.

Don't be disheartened if you find yourself doing exactly what you don't want to do. Time pressures and all sorts of other competing demands can take us off course from that place of presence. We all have hot spots that tip us from calm to reacting automatically.[28] Each time you notice yourself reacting in a way you regret, try to resist the urge to criticise yourself. Consider the fact you wouldn't chastise your friend for making the same mistake over and over. Self-compassion goes hand-in-hand with being mindful. If you are sitting on the fence about adopting a kinder response towards yourself, consider how far putting yourself down has taken you! How often do we tell ourselves that we will not tolerate that reaction and commit to not doing it again, only to find ourselves in the same position?

Finally, we've all had an embarrassing parenting moment such as when your child throws an almighty tantrum on the footpath or at a social gathering. You feel compelled to act quickly to prevent getting the onlookers' attention. Someone might even comment on what they think your child needs – such as discipline. To make matters worse let's consider you are shattered from dealing with numerous tantrums that day. How do you cope with your emotions and your child's while also dealing with what you perceive as the judgement from others? These types of challenging moments have a habit of coming up to test your new found approach.

Regardless of how you respond, take some time afterwards to debrief on your own or with someone. Reflect on what happened, what you did well, or what you could improve next time. Be like an investigator and look at what happened before the eruption. Get yourself to name your emotions and those of your child. Try to be objective and stick to the facts. Tell your friend you are trying this new approach to parenting. Perhaps you can support each other when you catch the other person being judgmental.

So, the next time you're feeling angry, anxious or guilty, or overwhelmed by a parenting moment, pause for a second and check-in with yourself. Get into the habit of asking yourself what your child is trying to tell you through their behaviour.

The wonderful thing about being a parent is that it is never too late to make changes to how you want to be with your child. We are all a product of our own parenting and the parenting of all the generations before us.

How compassionate are you towards yourself when you feel that old familiar pang of guilt that often follows a parenting moment that doesn't go so well? This sounds a bit gushy but inside us all is the need to be loved. Our children are a pure version of this as they have not built-up walls to fend off feelings of hurt that accumulate throughout a life time. Being able to parent in a way that provides space for your child to offload would surely be a more effective way to support them to deal with big emotions.

This is hard to do if your parenting taught you that it was unacceptable to be rude or to act out. Couple this with living in a culture that reinforces the reward punishment ethos, and it is easy to find yourself reacting to challenging behaviour.

Beneath your child's externalised behaviour is an unmet need, big emotions and a need to understand or be understood. The moment we are hooked into how displeased their behaviour makes us feel, it sends a message to them that it isn't safe to express whatever it is they are feeling. This can be applied if we react angrily to many behaviours, including relentless crying, food being thrown repeatedly on the ground, being told that the child hates you, hitting out at a sibling, and so on.

Before you embark on this monumental shift in your parenting style, start by looking at your own self-talk that we discussed previously. Do you show compassion to yourself when you find yourself repeating old habits you'd like to change? Remind yourself you are repeating what was most likely done to you. Chastising yourself only leads to an internalised form of self-punishment. You may not even be aware how natural it is for you to repeat old habits and put yourself down.

Another way of looking at it is putting yourself in the child's shoes and asking how you would like to be treated.

Start small and be prepared to put yourself into time-out so you can regroup and breath until you're ready to be there for your child no matter what is thrown at you.

Try out some of these practical strategies. It is a skill to master, so make time each day, when you feel relaxed, to practice. That way you will have skills to call on when feeling stressed.

Think of a stop sign the moment you notice yourself about to react. Pause. Take a breath. Notice what is happening in that moment (think body, thoughts, urges).

- Practice checking-in with what is happening for you and your child. Set yourself a check-in reminder twice a day and you'll be surprised how it helps you tune into the present.

- Apply a non-judgmental stance to everyday scenarios, such as the weather, to get better at being objective.

- Make time to practice being present doing tasks one at a time – such as the ones you do alone like brush your teeth and shower. Using your senses can help keep you in the present.

- Hold yourself to being good enough and not perfect, and notice when your thoughts are aiming too high.

Case in Point

A 21 year old mother had her first child through an unplanned pregnancy. The father of the child broke up with her when she told him about the pregnancy. He blamed her for being careless. She reported feeling resentful that all the financial burden and care of the baby was her responsibility. Prior to having the baby, this woman was studying full time and the last thing on her mind was becoming a mum. Her friends were busy partying and had tried to be supportive but they often asked her out at night when she felt too tired. Additionally she and the baby were living with her parents and she didn't want to burden them further by asking them to mind the baby when she went out.

Counselling involved helping her to see her blind spots – such as processing her feelings of anger about her life situation, validating her desire to return to stud, and assuring her she was not being selfish in wanting to have a career one day. She was encouraged to look at her upbringing and how it might be manifesting in the way she parented with low confidence, and also to look at how this was attached to her mother dominating the care of the baby.

Sessions included watching her play with her baby, during which there was an opportunity for modelling and supportive coaching so she could learn to tune into what her baby was saying with its body, facial expressions and vocalisations. She was counselled to change the activity accordingly or to take a break, and to understand this was not a sign of her being rejected by the baby but was instead a way of the baby communicating its needs ...

She was encouraged to make time each day to play with her baby on her own. She was also taught how to complete one minute mindfulness of her breathing and to practise this throughout the day. Accordingly, by counting 10 breaths, she was able to ground herself when she started to feel overwhelmed.

Her confidence increased with reading her babies cues and was further reinforced in sessions by validating real life examples. She was able to formulate her own version of being a mum, which was not being a housewife like her own mother, and she learnt it was acceptable to return to study and access onsite childcare for young mums.

To Recap

Old habits die hard. Your challenge now is to remember to practise mindful parenting. We need to try to correct patterns that have been handed down over many generations. Being tuned-in/mindful is the new age but it is possible to achieve it with the right amount of practice and encouragement. If you're feeling angry, anxious or guilty, or overwhelmed by a parenting moment, pause for a second and check-in with yourself. Get into the habit of asking yourself what your child is trying to tell you through their behaviour.

Your Turn

Actively tune into your child and ask yourself what are they trying to tell you.

Notice yourself operating from an unhelpful pattern and ask yourself how you would like to respond next time.

Awareness is power. Cue yourself to be present by adopting habits through reminders to be present.

Next

Bring it all together by arming yourself with a support network to help you to cope and not leave yourself depleted and expecting too much of yourself.

Chapter 12

Be Tuned-in To Others

You are not alone

THERE was never a truer statement than "it takes a community to raise a baby". Active steps are needed these days to build your own community support team. It is one of the final and most critical steps on your journey to calm. It is well researched that good social support for new parents promotes wellness, relationship satisfaction, child outcomes and stronger parent child interactions.[29]

Gone are the days that you can rely on your neighbour to drop off a cooked meal or mind your baby with a moment's notice. Can you imagine staying in hospital for two whole weeks after giving birth? So much has changed in the past fifty years. By the time you went home you had established your baby's feeding and sleep routine. Maternal child health provided a drop-in service where you could visit any time you had a question.

There was also no social media flashing up on your phone to spread the word about the latest celebrity returning to her svelte pre-pregnancy figure in two weeks to set the benchmark that you failed to meet. It is not surprising there is mixed results for time spent on the internet, and that social networking and subscribing to "mummy blogs" have opened up new doors to access information and a sense of connection.[30] However, social media can promote stress if used to compare self to others or to receive unsupportive comments when you share your updates or opinions with your following.

Some cultures today still adopt practices to help ensure mums rest after birth. For example, in a Greek family the mother is expected to stay home for 40 days. During this time close family and friends visit to care for mum and baby. It is very effective, as mothers don't feel bad taking time out to be looked after.

The western world has the opposite approach and makes no allowances for birth recovery. Time to simply feed your baby – is there such a thing, you might ask. How do you access the right peer support and mentoring to ease the transition? In reality, it is every woman for herself.

Some of you will be lucky to have partners on leave, supportive family and friendship networks that naturally step in and help out. It is important to consider the judgments you hold about asking for help. Do you consider it acceptable, or is it a sign of not coping or incompetence?

Mothering is a long-haul occupation and support needs change along the way. A support network is different for every mum and needs to be reviewed from time-to-time as children grow and you change.

When is the last time you considered what your support needs are? Perhaps you don't know where to start. Read on and you'll have your own survival guide to meeting your needs by the end of this chapter.

So far you have learnt about the importance of meeting the

body's physical needs, reconnected with your interests outside of being a mum, and started practicing ways to calm the farm by adopting self-soothing and with fact-checking skills.

As you can see, there is a lot you are able to do yourself to optimise wellbeing and mastery of this mothering gig.

As human beings we are social. Whether you consider yourself an introvert or extrovert, everyone needs a robust support system, tailored to our individual needs, and which we can rely on without making us feel uncomfortable about using the support people.

Here are some things to consider:

Practical support

Do you have family living nearby? Geography matters and some people move after having kids to be closer to support who can help out with raising the kids.

Are you on top of cooking and cleaning? It's okay to outsource.

Social support

Have your friends had kids? Or are they interested in kids? It can be isolating being the only couple in your social group who has a baby/child.

Do you need to form new social networks with other parents?

Are you part of a parent support group who all had kids about the same time? It can be a powerful connector to be on the same journey even though you might not have other things in common. Don't be afraid to try other pathways such as council-run playgroups or kid-friendly clubs/activities/venues.

Do you have someone you can call to have fun with? I know

right, I said fun! Go out dancing with maybe – do something that doesn't involve children.

Personal Support

Do you have a trusted friend/person you can count on whenever you need to vent or seek advice? Fear of judgment from others gets in the way of sharing our most coveted selves. It is unlikely anyone will ever judge you as harshly as you do.

Who can you call on to babysit at the last minute? Someone you don't feel bad asking because you know you can reciprocate.

Professional Support

Who is your health support team for you and your family?

Do you have a regular family-friendly GP?

Do you have any other health professionals you need – such as paediatrician, maternal child health nurse, teachers, and counsellors?

> **Case in Point**
>
> *A 41 year old mother of a two week old baby had a partner who worked full-time in a new job, and had no leave. All her immediate family lived interstate. Her baby was diagnosed with colic, and was only comforted by being held in an upright position. Prior to having a baby, this woman held a senior accountant's role, and was used to achieving work targets. Her friends were younger when they had children and were at a different phase in their parenting.*
>
> *Counselling involved helping her see her blind spots – such as her career had reinforced her need for perfectionism, order and control. She was advised to look at how her traits might be manifested in the way she handled her*

baby's feed/sleep routine, and how she dealt with an unsettled baby.

She was encouraged to go to different health professionals to cure the baby's pain, and to change her diet to make her breast milk more digestible for her baby. She was asked to look at whether she was staying up too late or not resting enough while she tried to catch up with domestic tasks. The suggestion that she find someone nearby, in the same boat, to confide in and to validate her proved very helpful. Problem-solving her time-use saw her hiring a cleaner, having ready-made meals for a few nights a week, and discussing with her husband what she needed help with. They agreed that, despite his working, he could manage to complete chores and take the baby out to give her a break. By setting up a more manageable routine, it made husband and wife feel closer and he enjoyed a closer relationship with their child …

To Recap

Having a support system to help out with personal, social, practical and health needs prevents you from burn out and allows you to have a balanced life where you can go out on your own and seek out advice to keep you in check.

Your Turn

Answer the questions and assign who your people are. It's okay if you don't have it all covered. It becomes your plan for what you may need to source.

Next

We're up to the final word. Let's do a quick summary of what you've learnt and hopefully the things you are putting into practice.

The Final Word
You Have the Information

Now you can make calm your default state

IF you've been practising the tasks mapped out in this book, you now have the skills you need to find the state of calm you seek, and to have mastered this mum-ability business (at least as well as any of us can).

Here's a summary:

Your emotions are not the boss of you. Reduce your vulnerability by taking the time to meet your own needs – attend to PLEASE self-care needs.

Deal with time management demands by swapping perfection for acceptance that you can't always do everything you would like to do. The only way to save time is to prioritise and delegate.

Discover yourself by connecting with your values so you have clarity about what is important to you and what motivates you.

Know that how you react to that bond with your baby depends on the bonds created in your own childhood. You might have a secure attachment to your baby – or maybe an anxious attachment or an avoidant attachment.

Look into your past to understand why you react the way you do to your child. We often continue the parenting styles of our mother and her mother before her.

Being able to name our emotions and pinpoint the triggers for them is, in essence, what we need to be able to do to take charge of managing emotions. Figuring out what exactly you are feeling and why can be complicated, yet it is an important skill to be able to accurately interpret how you feel, and also to be able to express yourself clearly to others.

Our thoughts are not necessarily based on actual facts. It causes us stress when we react to those thoughts in ways that are not what we wanted to do as a parent. Often, we're perpetuating behaviours our parents used in rearing us.

Good problem-solving skills turn problems into possible solutions. Whether it's deciding to return to work, or whether you should be saying no instead of yes, or how to curb your yelling, or any of the many problems that arise during parenting, look at the pros and cons of changing behaviour to help you address unhelpful patterns or to be better able to make difficult decisions.

It isn't always easy to ask for what you want, to give feedback when someone upsets you, or to say no to a request. Don't get caught up in worrying about how other people perceive you.

Next

This book is designed to be a practical guide to new mums and to mums who already have children.

Dip into this book again whenever you need to. It never hurts to sharpen your skills.

Share the book (and maybe your experiences) with someone you think needs to read it.

ACKNOWLEDGEMENTS

Thank you to all those who encouraged me and helped move me from procrastination into making the time to write this book.

I could not have written the book without the unwavering technical support of copyeditor (and my mother-in-law) Michele McCormack. She finessed my words, provided copious structural advice and spent hours on my drafts to enable me to publish this, my first book.

My grateful thanks also to Deb Carrin, Manager of the Hume Community Team, who wrote the Foreword for this book. It was Deb who facilitated my journey into the specialist field of postnatal therapy, and gave me the tools to build on my knowledge base, which I've shared here with readers of this book.

About the Author

Therapist and Mumability blogger Ginny Hartley's first career was as an occupational therapist. Ginny said it was a natural progression from there to her next career as a counsellor and therapist. She continued to work, acquiring additional skills and tools to advance her career while adding to her academic qualifications. Today, her career has stretched across more than 20 years of mental health practice, specialising in postnatal work.

Professionally, Ginny is passionate about helping mums enjoy motherhood. She is eager to share the insights into motherhood she gained via her studies, career and practice, and she wants to see mothers own their own version of being a mum, through unpacking their past and upskilling.

Privately, mother-of-two Ginny treasures family life and loves nothing better than entertaining her large family and wide circle of friends. Ever mindful of practicing what she preaches, Ginny sets aside "me" time where she works out, runs, trains for marathons and chills out with yoga. Part of her regime is to bicycle 20-plus km, each day, to and from her job in whatever weather conditions are thrown at her. Living in a private haven by the Yarra River in a home backing onto a natural bush park, Ginny and her family love the outdoor existence and the fact that they are only a few kilometres from all the action that Melbourne offers.

Journey to Calm is Ginny's first book.

www.mumability.com.au

DISCLAIMER

The author has made every effort to ensure that the information in this book was correct at the time of publication. However, the author and publisher accept no liability for any loss, damage or disruption incurred by the reader or any other person arising from any action taken or not taken based on the content of this book. The author recommends seeking third party advice and considering all options prior to making any decision or taking action in regard to the content of this book.

REFERENCES

[1] Lineham, M. (2015). DBT Skills Training Manual (second edition): New York: The Guilford Press.

[2] healthdirect.gov.au.

[3] Novak, V. Sugar and the brain. Harvard and Mahoney Neuroscience Institute on the brain newsletter.

[4] Mitchell, H.H. Journal of Biological Chemistry 158.

[5] Horne, J. (2006).Sleep faring: A journey through the science of sleep. Amazon.

[6] Collins, R. (2017). Exercise, depression and the brain. July 25. Health line.

[7] betterhealth channel.vic.gov.au.

[8] Rose, J. (April 2017) Never enough hours in the day: employed mothers' perceptions of time pressure, Australian Journal of Social Issues.

[9] Asp, K. (2013) How to claim some "ME time". Webmd Oct 23 2013.

[10] Cherry, K. (2020) How multitasking affects productivity and brain health. Very well mind. 26 March 2020.

[11] Farber, N. (2012). The value of goals. Psychology Today. April 19 2012.

[12] Bowlby, J as cited in McLeod, S.A. (2017). Mary Ainsworth. The strange situation attachment styles. Simply Psychology.org.

[13] McLeod, S.A. (2017). Mary Ainsworth. The strange situation attachment styles. Simply Psychology.org.

[14] Woodhouse et al. (2020). Secure base provision: A new link approach to examining links between maternal caregiving and infant attachment. Society for Research in Child development .Pubmed.gov.

[15] Fraiberg, S. (1975). Ghosts in the Nursery: A Psychoanalytic Approach to the Problems on Impaired Infant-Mother Relationships. Journal of American Academy of Child Psychiatry. Summer 1975 p 387-421

[16] Abblett, M. (2019). Tame reactive emotions by naming them. Mindful. 25 Sep 2019

[17] Lenzen, M. 2005). Feeling our emotions. Scientific American Journal April 1 2005.

[18] Craske, M. as cited in Aldao, A. (2014). Why labelling emotions matters. Psychology.

[19] Champagne, T. (2008). Sensory Modulation and the environment: essential elements of occupation (3rd edition). South Hampton MA.

[20] Goldman, D. (1995). Emotional intelligence: why it can matter more than IQ. New York. Bantam books.

[21] National Science Foundation (2005) Thoughts a Day1 1.

[22] Cuncic, A. (2020). Negative automatic thoughts and social anxiety. Very well mind. Sept 17 2020.

[23] Zemen, E. 2019). How to Check the facts. Mind soother therapy centre. 15 December 2019.

[24] Shokoohi-Yekta, M., Parand,A., Zamani, N., Lotfi, S. & Ayazi, M. (2011). Teaching problem solving for parents: effects on children's misbehaviour. Sviverse Science direct (30) p 163–166.

[25] Speed, B.C., Goldstein, B.L. & Goldfried, M.R. (2018) Assertiveness training: A forgotten evidence based treatment. Clinical Psychology: Science and Practise 25(1) Wiley Online Library.

[26] Syaodih, E. & Handayani, H. (2016). Development Assertive Ability of young children as a counter measure effort for bullying behaviour.

[27] Race, K (2014) Mindful Parenting: Simple and Powerful Solutions for Raising Creative, Engaged, Happy Kids in Today's Hectic World.

[28] Race, K (2014) Mindful Parenting: Simple and Powerful Solutions for Raising Creative, Engaged, Happy Kids in Today's Hectic World.

[29] McDaniel, B.T., Holmes, E.K. & Coyne, S. (2011) New mothers and media use: associations between blogging, social networking, and maternal well-being. Maternal and Child Health Journal. PuBmed Research Gate.

[30] McDaniel, B.T., Holmes, E.K. & Coyne, S. (2011) New mothers and media use: associations between blogging, social networking, and maternal well-being. Maternal and Child Health Journal. PuBmed Research Gate.

www.ingramcontent.com/pod-product-compliance
Ingram Content Group UK Ltd.
Pitfield, Milton Keynes, MK11 3LW, UK
UKHW022225230426
12048UKWH00016BA/1058